Wealthy Child
Financial Success for the Children in Your Life

William A. Gerosa

Copyright © William A. Gerosa 2007

All rights reserved. No part of this publication may be reproduced or transmitted in any form or by any means, electronic or mechanical, including photocopy, recording or any information and retrieval system, without permission in writing from the copyright holder/publisher, except in the case of brief quotations embodied in critical articles reviews.

ISBN 978-0-6152-4172-2

Published in the United States by Convergence Technologies, Inc.

www.GroWWealthy.com

To Kim. You make everything possible.

To Nicole, Grace and all children. May you master personal finance and use it to accomplish all you wish in life.

Contents

Introduction

How Children Learn About Money
What Is Money?
Don't Make These Mistakes
The Five Pillars
Pillar One: Earn
Pillar One: Earning and the Later Years
Pillar Two: Save
The Rule of No Credit
The Savings Box
The Age Old Battle: Needs vs. Wants
Exercise Discipline and Delay Gratification
Advertising
The Power of Advertising
Track, Track, Track Your Expenses
Pillar Three: Time to Invest and Grow
Nothing But Time
The Penny Game
A Good Example for Your Child
How to Invest for Your Child Early
How Your Child's Funds Should Be Invested
What to Expect
Invest on a Regular Basis
The Importance of Doing Nothing
Pillar Four: Multiple Streams of Income
Residential Rental Properties
Commercial Properties
Tax Free Money and the 1031 Exchange
Web Based and Small Businesses

Investing in Other Businesses
The Best Tax Break Around: Owning a Business
Other Thoughts on Multiple Streams of Income
Pillar Five: Wealth Building
Financial Precision
Your Child and Retirement Plans
Never Buy Depreciating Assets on Credit
About Credit Cards
Your Child's Credit Score
Poor Credit History or No Credit History
The Family Business
Investing With Your Younger Child
Investing With Your Older Child
UTMAs and UGMAs – Getting the Best Deal
The Dangers of Your Child Having Money
The Worker and The Capitalist
The Money Game
Good and Bad Debt
Kid Friendly Businesses
More on the Roth IRA
Live at Home
Buy a Home as Soon as Possible
How to Buy the Right Home, Not Too Big, Not Too Small
College
Tracking Your Net Worth
Wills, Guardians, Life Insurance, Trusts and Other Fun Topics
The Fourteen Rules of Wealth

Appendix
About the Author

Introduction

The modern world is very interesting place. As the day of our first daughter's birth grew nearer I began to think about where she would be in three decades. I thought about how well off she would be and the path that would lead her there. I thought back on my own life over the past three decades. During that time I had a few financial successes, many missed opportunities and several financial failures. I would be far better off today if I had access to greater knowledge from the time I was twenty years old. It was after this period of thinking and the knowledge that our daughter was to be born in a few months that I decided to teach her, from an early age, about money and wealth. This teaching would be very important for her as well as all of the other things she would need, such as love, education and self respect. I wanted her to have the greatest chance of being healthy and happy in the future. I believe that the goal for each person is to live well and help others live well. In my opinion, living well requires health, family, happiness and a certain degree of wealth.

This book does not contain any quick fixes, secrets of the rich, tips to magically turn your child's financial life around or any golden rules. If there were any shortcuts I can assure you I would have discovered them by now. Wealthy Child contains a program that is a common sense approach to learning about and mastering the financial side of the world we live in. You should not be looking for quick fixes or secrets of the rich and famous. I can tell you now that there are none.

What truly amazes me about interviews with self made millionaires is how ordinary these people are. Occasionally, there is a millionaire who has a great story about how she made her money. These edge of your chair stories are few and far between. Most wealthy people have built their wealth by working hard and paying attention to the little details. They just went out and did it. They earned money by working hard. They saved religiously and they worked hard at growing their wealth. This is what you should teach your child as she grows in the years to come. This is what Wealthy Child will help you and your child achieve. This is far too important area of life to leave to chance.

Wealthy Child is a stepping stone that covers many topics and will provide you with a roadmap for greatly increasing your child's chances of financial success. Many topics will be covered in great detail and others will only be given a brief mention. You should research, in greater depth any topic that you feel is of particular interest to you and your child. One major facet of financial well being is ongoing education. You may find additional information on the internet and may want to obtain books from your library or from online booksellers that cover a specific topic, such as 529 College Savings Plans.

During this journey with your child keep in mind that it is very important that you have your own financial house in order. Before you are able to help your children you will need to have your own finances properly arranged and have a plan for the future. At the very least this includes saving, saving for retirement, having a will and other critical documents in place and understanding the relationships between all facets of your financial life. Many parents will forgo their own financial well being to help their children. Many parents will save money for their child's education and at the same time will not save anything for their own retirement. This is not an optimal strategy.

Keep in mind the if your child is doing well as a young adult and must help you financially because of poor planning on your part this situation could negatively effect his financial position. No parent wants this to happen. Do what you need to do to address any shortcomings in your current financial situation. Meet with a financial planner. Set goals and deadlines for your savings plan and for meeting important financial issues. Many of the topics and ideas presented in Wealthy Child apply to adults as well and hopefully you will be able to apply the information to your own financial life.

If there is one concept that I urge you and your child to truly take to heart while reading Wealthy Child it is striving to understand the difference between knowing and doing. Why is this point so important? It is far too easy to read a book such as Wealthy Child and say to yourself, "I learned a few things reading the book but most of it seemed like common sense," and then put the book on the bookshelf and never think of it again.

Wealthy people understand that there is a huge difference between knowing and doing. Why do you think that very successful business people attend business seminars or star athletes review their golf swings or jump shots with coaches? It is not because these people need to learn these skills. They already have these skills! However, they acknowledge that even though they know they may not be doing. While knowledge (knowing) is a critical first step to achieving anything if we don't act on the knowledge and get down to doing nothing will happen. Please always keep in mind the difference between knowing and doing and spend a lot of time doing.

Thank you for purchasing Wealthy Child and feel free to email us with questions and we will do our best to reply in a timely manner. You may also purchase additional copies of this book at our website, listed below. Our email address is Comments@GroWWealthy.com and you may visit our website at www.GroWWealthy.com to learn more about personal finance, investing and growing wealth. Our aim is to help you, help yourself and your children with money and wealth.

Throughout his book I will use the word child. I, of course, refer to any and all children that you may have in your life. I will also use him and her, interchangeably, to refer to your child or children simply to avoid undue repetition.

Please keep in mind that this book is not all encompassing and purposely omits certain details for the sake of communicating broad ideas to help you and your child. This book should not be taken as financial advice and makes no such representation. Please seek the help of a qualified and competent financial professional as you investigate topics that interest you.

"There are two ways to be rich: want less or earn more."

How Children Learn About Money

Luckily, I picked up mostly good, and a few very bad, money habits from my own family as I grew up. I learned to earn money and save, almost to the point of obsession. My family was insistent that all of the children receive at least a college level education.

Even with all of the good lessons I learned from my family about money, I did not learn how to grow those savings and how to create wealth. This is what tends to separate the wealthy from the middle class. I had learned only two of the "Five Pillars" needed to build significant wealth and income. I was able to recover from this lack of knowledge later in life by studying economics and finance and working in financial services.

I wanted my daughter to master and understand all Five Pillars so that she would have the greatest chance of succeeding and leading a full life. I wanted her to learn these skills early enough in life so that she could avoid the many, many pitfalls that entrap young people today and so that she would be able to take advantage of financial opportunities that would certainly cross her path in the future.

Shortly after deciding to help my daughter, I began talking to and teaching young people about money. It amazed me what they did and did not know. I live in a neighborhood with a fair number of very well educated people. Some of them hold multiple college and graduate level degrees. Their children learn calculus, inorganic chemistry and ancient Greek. However, their children's lack of knowledge when it came to money was staggering. There no longer appear to be home economics classes taught in school. We all have heard the urban legend about the child, when asked where money comes from, replies, "The ATM machine!" Most children do not know what a checkbook is. They do not know what a loan is or how one works. There was a study that showed that most college students do not know the difference between a stock and a bond. This is a generation that will have to save for their retirement as the traditional pension plan has been disappearing at a rapid rate. The world will require greater financial knowledge from your child than from any previous generation.

It is lack of knowledge that makes children and young adults prey for a host of dangers such as overspending, getting into credit card debt and blindly taking loans without thinking through the range of financial consequences. It is a lack of knowledge that allows young adults to take on mortgages that are too large and forces them to struggle for years because they can barely make ends meet. Years ago it was almost impossible to get into financial trouble because the world was simpler and no one would lend you more money than you could afford to pay back. There were far fewer difficult to understand financial offerings such as Adjustable Rate Mortgages (ARMs).

It is somewhat ironic. Our society is obsessed by money. By far the most important things in life are health, happiness, family and being thankful. Money helps to make life easier, no doubt about it, but our society often forgets what is most important. For all of the obsessing about money, our kids know almost nothing about what money is, how to earn it, how to keep it and how to make it grow.

I hope that this book helps you help your child to live a happier and more financially rewarding life. I hope it brings you closer to your child and engenders a feeling of empowerment in your child as he or she enjoys mastering something that for too many people masters them.

What Is Money?

Let's stop for a moment and think about the definition of money. The dictionary states that, "money is any good or token that is used in trade as a medium of exchange, store of value, and unit of account." OK, that is not very helpful as the definition was probably written by an economist and will not help you teach your six year old son about money.

Just as your child learns the alphabet and learns to count, the best way to teach him about money is to show him the different coins such as the quarter, dime, nickel and penny along with several different bills. Review with him the difference between each and how a dollar represents four quarters, ten dimes and twenty nickels. This lesson is not easy for children as it requires a certain level of mathematics. The best way to teach your children about money is to expose them to money and how money is used in daily life.

Let your child pay for groceries when you get to the checkout counter. Let him receive the change from the cashier. Discuss with your child the transaction that just occurred. Let him look at the receipt and the figures associated with each grocery item. Your child does not need to understand exactly what is going on, but being exposed to the process will help him in the future have a framework for learning more about money.

Explain to him how money was created. Long ago, people exchanged their services and goods by a system of barter. If you were good at fixing roofs and I raised healthy cattle, you would fix my roof and I would give you one of my best cattle. The problem with this system is that it entailed a high "search cost." I needed to find someone who was good at fixing roofs and wanted one head of cattle.

The other problem with this system is that many of the goods that people were willing to exchange for other things of value would not keep. Think of the corn farmer. His crop would come to harvest and he had only a very small window within which he could trade his fresh corn for other goods and services.

Money was invented to establish a common unit of value for the exchange of goods and services. I could sell my cattle as I liked and receive money for this transaction. Then when my roof needed to be repaired, I would pay someone in money to fix my roof. While not perfect, the system of money was a vast improvement over the previous barter system.

As your child grows older and is able to work with numbers have him track his net worth from time to time. He should add up the money he has plus other things of value. At this time your child is unlikely to have any debts or liabilities so drawing up a net worth statement will be easy.

To strengthen their understanding of money, play the Money Game as described later in this book with your children. It is a lot of fun and will help them understand the different units of money. It will also familiarize them with the transactions of buying and selling.

Always keep in mind that your children will listen to what you explain to them and they will retain, sometimes without immediately understanding, a tremendous amount of this information. However, your behavior with respect to money is what you children will truly pay attention to. The lesson: if you have some "problems" in your relationship with money please take this opportunity to correct them.

Don't Make These Mistakes

One big and very common mistake most families make is not talking about money at all. In some families discussing money, income and net worth is considered dirty. Each family will find what level of disclosure is comfortable for them. Money was never discussed in my family. I believe that children should be given some insight into family finances, depending on their age. It may be something as simple as helping budget for the weekly grocery shopping.

Another very common mistake is treating money with a sense of paranoia and fear. This often leads to the hording mentality and a general distaste for financial matters. Most of us know someone like this. They refuse to spend money at any cost. They wear rags and would rather sit and stare at a wall all day long than spend a dime. This mentality within a family usually creates children who act like their parents and this creates stress in their lives because they continually deprive themselves of even the smallest pleasures in life. Sometimes a family that thinks this way about money creates spendthrift children. "My old man was terribly cheap and I am never going to live that way." This is not good either because these children usually spend everything they earn and sometimes more.

A very common mistake is to treat money as if it were evil. If you think something is evil the tendency is to avoid it whenever possible. Ignoring money is very much like ignoring other things in life. Generally, we are better off when we address life's issues in a timely manner rather than ignoring them. When we ignore important aspects of life, it comes back to haunt us with a vengeance. Don't consider money evil. Money is neither evil nor good. You will often hear people state, "The bible says that 'money is the root of all evil.'" This is an incorrect statement. The bible actually says, "For the love of money is the root of all evil."

It is what you and I do with money and how we act in obtaining it that is good or evil. The analogy I always use is that of a hammer. No one considers a hammer "good" or "bad." A hammer is simply a lifeless object. You may use a hammer to build a house, which most people would consider good, or you may use a hammer to break someone's hand, which most of us would consider bad.

Another big mistake is focusing too much on money and often times in the wrong way. Some parents exert tremendous pressure on their children to earn a lot of money. Sometimes these parents push children into professions that are not a good fit.

The worst part of this thinking is that it usually only focuses on the first of the Five Pillars, earning money. Well, we all know it is not what you earn that really matters, it is what you keep. There are so many casualties of the "earn a lot save a little syndrome" that I could not even begin to provide a list. Professional athletes who must declare bankruptcy, doctors and lawyers getting themselves into debt to the point of no return and regular working families living beyond their means.

The best way for your children to treat money is to learn about it so that they see money as a means to achieve and accomplish the things in life they want. It is a lot like the relationship we have with our cars. For most of us our cars are a method of getting us where we want to go. If used properly, cars greatly expand our quality of life. If used improperly a car can greatly reduce the quality of our life or even end it. The best way to use a car is to respect the dangers that a car can create, use it responsibly and enjoy the privilege of using a car. A car needs to be maintained and understood to a certain degree to avoid problems and to provide best service. Your child should develop the same healthy mastery of money. Money should not be feared and it should not be worshipped. It is something we need to live so we should learn how best to use it to our advantage.

The Five Pillars

Most of life is rather simple in theory, but complex in practice. The same is true of money and personal finance. A lot of money has been made through gambling, the lottery, a hot stock, inheritance, get rich quick schemes and a whole host of other shortcuts. While these methods of gaining wealth are highly publicized, the stark truth is that most wealthy people did not achieve their wealth in any of these ways. They earned what they have. Unfortunately, our children never hear these stories of steady, continuous earning and saving. Even if our kids did hear these stories they are not nearly as exciting as tales of overnight riches. It is our responsibility to teach our children the most likely way to obtain financial security and freedom. Just as we teach them to eat properly, respect others and do their schoolwork, we must teach them the most likely path to wealth.

Working, saving and investing. Investing, saving and working. Repeating this process leads to wealth. Now, I know this is no fun because it means work and work is not nearly as fun to a child as scratching a lottery card and walking home with a bag of money. Once your child has mastered the basics of wealth building there are plenty of opportunities to embrace risk and potentially build wealth quickly but it is always best to learn to walk first before trying to run.

So, if the most predictable path to wealth is by small, progressive steps over time, also known as work, then this is where we should start. If your child is lucky enough to win the lottery or become a professional athlete along the way, even better. And, your child will know how to handle that money because he has mastered the basics. Most wealthy people have followed a well known and predictable path. They have learned the Five Pillars of Wealth. They are:

Pillar One: Earn

Pillar Two: Save

Pillar Three: Time (Invest and Grow)

Pillar Four: Multiple Streams of Income

Pillar Five: Wealth Building

Don't underestimate the importance of teaching your children Pillar One. This is where it all begins. Many kids have no idea where money comes from or how to obtain it.

I know a husband and wife with two children. The parents are both very bright, very loving and they are also Certified Public Accountants (CPAs). At the time, the oldest child was nearly sixteen. We will call him David. The mother was telling me that David had no concept of money and was simply given $100 every time he wanted to go to the mall. When I asked why the child of two CPAs knew nothing about money at an age where I had been working two jobs, the mother replied, "Oh, we want him to focus on school and not on working for money."

Now, in five years when David is nearly ready to graduate college, has been bombarded by credit card offers for almost two years and faces making his own way in the world, do you think he will get himself into financial trouble? I do. And, I think David could be one of those young adults who wakes up one day and is thirty years old with no savings and a pile of debt. Even if David does not get into financial trouble in the years to come there is still a good chance that his financial progress will be held back by lack of knowledge.

All of the knowledge that you and I have acquired about money and how it works cannot be taken for granted. We do not assume that our children will learn how to speak or how to read as they grow up. We take active steps to ensure that these vital skills are learned as our sons and daughters grow. Why should we assume that children will automatically learn how to handle money? In fact, the evidence is showing us that young people have no idea how to handle their own finances.

We cannot assume that our children will learn the proper ways to deal with money from friends, teachers and the media. Children see money the way an English only speaker enjoys an Italian Opera. The opera observer has some idea as to what is going on, but not understanding Italian he misses much of the detail and so much of success in any area of life boils down to the details. Make it a point to teach your children that:

Money is like any other valued resource. You must work, in some way shape or form, to obtain it. Instill in your children the notion that work is good. Urge them to find something that they really enjoy and then work really isn't "work" and they will earn money doing what they love. School and further education is the surest and safest way to more income and a greater ability to earn money and create wealth.

A part time job is one of the best ways your child will learn about money. While school should be your child's number one mission there is nothing like a part time job or a summer job to teach them the value of dollar and how to get along with others in the workplace.

Teach them that money, in and of itself, really has no value. Its value lies in its ability to allow you to buy things and do the things you want in life. Money also creates mental comfort. If you have enough money in the bank to get you through two years of living expenses then you are less likely to worry about money, unemployment and where your next paycheck will come from.

Pillar One: Earn

Although it is obvious, in order to save money and build wealth you must first earn money. You must have some way of trading your skill, or capital or both, in return for money. Children do not automatically understand this.

As your child grows up as part of your family a great lesson for her to learn is the value of work. At first, she will work not for money, but because work is part of life and it helps the family.

I believe that an important precursor to teaching your children about money and finance is that they understand work. Your child should have a set of chores that he or she is responsible for completing each week. As your child learns to take on chores and the responsibility that you place in him, he will also slowly learn that chores (work) have a value because work gets things done. Work is what allows the family to have a nice dinner at the end of the day. Work is what allows us to have clean clothes each morning. I am sure that you can find things that your child enjoys and link that enjoyment to work.

Children as young as two are able to help with simple chores. At the age of 20 months, my daughter had a few, small chores. She helped moving laundry from one area to the laundry bin. For some reason she showed an interest in cleaning up and moving laundry, so we started there.

Of course, young children do not understand that this is work or the concept of chores. They do these things because they are imitating us and/or they find some fun in doing so. That is fine as a start. Let your child help by doing some repetitive physical activity where you can show them that his efforts help you or others. In time, you can tackle the mental concept of work and chores and how this helps the family.

As your child continues to help with chores, you should introduce him to the concept of being paid for <u>additional work</u>. In other words, everyone in the family has chores that they must complete, free of charge, simply because that is the way families work. If the parent or parents did not go to work every day, if the grocer did not have food for purchase, if the electric company did not do their job and provide electricity our world would be much less fun. This is also why your child should tend to his or her chores.

Once your child is continually completing their chores for the family, they may take on additional work for money. This can be a routine job, such as emptying all of the waste paper baskets each week, or a one time project such as painting a picnic table. The important task for the parent is to convey that good work will have value to someone else who will be willing to pay you to do that work. This is the first step to Pillar One.

Most children find the prospect of earning money fun and initially become very excited. However, young children have a limited ability to focus and may quickly become distracted and disinterested. Be very careful, whether it is with chores or with paid work, not to assign or let your child take on tasks that will be destined for failure. It is much better for the parent to let the child take on a task that is a little too easy rather than too hard. The child should feel a sense of accomplishment in completing chores and paid work.

These chores and paid work should all be very small in scale and should take a small amount of the child's time each day and each week. It is not terribly important how long the chore or paid work takes, but it is very important that these chores and paid work are part of the child's regular routine.

Let's summarize what we have covered so far by age group:

Ages 2 through 4: Children should be asked to help with very simple tasks. They should help to carry things. They should help in cleaning up their play areas. During this time they should be shown that their work helps the family and that you appreciate what they are doing. Even when children of this age make a mess or actually create more work by helping, you must be positive and encourage them. Since children of this age cannot handle most chores themselves, it will have to be a group activity with at least one parent helping.

Ages 4 through 6: Children of this age are beginning to understand the concept of chores and that they are truly helping the family. They should have regularly scheduled chores that they will be expected to remember and complete on their own. It is often helpful to create a calendar with them so that they are able to see by week what chores they are responsible for handling. For example, if they are expected to empty the garbage in their room each Tuesday, this can be placed on their calendar.

Children of this age also are ready to begin paid work. Along with The Money Game (covered later), this paid work will accomplish several things. First, your child will begin to understand the difference between chores that help the family and additional paid work. Second, the child will begin to learn the concept of work for pay. She should learn that work has value and that value may be traded for money. She will also begin to learn that the money that she earns has value as well and may be traded for other things of value such as toys. Third, you may now begin to introduce your child to the concept of saving. This will be covered later under Pillar Two, but a child of this age should be made to save 50% of each dollar he or she earns.

Ages 6 through 11: Children of this age should have chores mastered and will be able to take on new and varied chores relatively easily once shown. Physically, doing chores is not much of a problem for children this age. However, they will often resist saying that chores are no fun and that they won't do them. This is where the constant repetition and discipline will go a long way in addressing this resistance. I am also a firm believer in treating children like adults. Ask them why they don't like chores. Tell them how much their chores help the family and how much their help is appreciated. A child of this age still finds his parent or parents the center of the universe and will do almost anything to please them. Ask them what would happen if you didn't feel like preparing dinner or paying the electric bill.

Children between the ages of 6 and 11 also will be able to partake of some of the "Child Friendly Businesses" we cover later and will be able to handle paid work for neighbors. This is a very important step because children will come to learn that other people, besides their family, depend on them to do certain things. Much of what a child is able to do at these ages depends on the child and her strengths and weaknesses. Simply expose them to as much as possible and get a feeling for what they like and dislike. You'll quickly learn their strengths and weaknesses.

If you have a family business, you may want to involve your child in the business to some limited degree. They will begin to learn a little about business, they can be paid for some simple work and you will be able to spend a little time with them during the day. You may also want to consider another one of our publications, *Roth IRAs for Youngsters*, where, as a business owner, you can create a retirement plan for your son or daughter that will be worth hundreds of thousand if not millions of dollars (and these are tax free dollars) in 20, 30 or 40 years.

Ages 11 through 15: Children between the ages of 11 and 15 will be able to take on more complicated and lengthy work for pay. Many times children of this age group will want to work more than you are comfortable with. They should be taught the importance of work for pay but you must continue to reinforce the notion that school is their primary task as it will allow them to obtain jobs in the future that will pay many times what they are earning currently. Your child should learn that he always needs to focus on doing things today that have the greatest long term benefit.

This is also the age where you can step beyond the "Child Friendly Businesses" and test the waters to see if your child has an entrepreneurial bent. Like many other abilities, it appears that entrepreneurs have some genetic traits that give them an advantage, but those who study business leaders and entrepreneurs also know that much of this behavior and these abilities are learned. If you are a business owner or have access to a family business this is the age at which you really will be able to involve your son or daughter.

This also is an age range where your child's views on money, working and saving will begin to solidify. This is a period where the habits they learn, either consciously or unconsciously, either from you or from the TV, will really begin to dictate their behavior in the decades to come. Some of their thinking on these topics will be based on their personality and is probably genetic, some of it will come from their friends, TV and popular culture, but the overwhelming force will be what they learn at home from their family.

Continue to teach them the importance of working and earning a living. Begin to stress that work is something that is part of life and that even retirement in the traditional sense is slowly disappearing as people live longer and many find that they continue to work because they enjoy it.

Try to determine what types of work your child does and does not like. Get them to discover for themselves what kinds of work they enjoy. Talk with them about what they would like to do when they get older. Ask them how they envision themselves in 10 or 20 years (see more on this below under Pillar One: Earning and the Later Years).

Children within this age range should be able to track their income throughout the year and keep a log of how much they earned along with the date and the reason for those earnings. A notebook or even a computer spreadsheet should be maintained by your child in any form that you and he agree upon.

Keeping track of income may seem like a simple, time wasting procedure, but it is very beneficial. Most people do not apply financial precision to their lives. They have some idea about how much money they earn, less of an idea about the total dollar amount of taxes they pay in a year and almost no idea how much money they spend, broken down by category. As we will discuss later, without a certain level of financial precision it is impossible to determine one's progress, good or bad, and does not allow for course corrections or improvements. Lacking financial precision in one's personal accounting also does not allow one to take advantage of financial opportunities that arise. Make sure that your child begins to track his income in some way throughout the year.

Ages 15 through 21: This age range covers a pretty wide span and the difference of one year during this period of your child's life can make a big difference. It is also the time when many children head off to college and/or begin working.

You should continue the lessons that you have been teaching your child all along. You should see a very pronounced difference in your child's level of financial maturity in comparison to his peers.

However, there are still many financial dangers lurking around the corner. As will be covered later in the book, this is an age where we will introduce your child to many other financial topics, such as investing, buying a home, avoiding debt and credit cards and building wealth. Hopefully, as they reach their 20th birthday, your child will have mastered the First Pillar of Wealth.

Pillar One: Earning and the Later Years

As your child progresses through her early teen years you have already tried to determine what type of work he or she enjoys. You should discuss various careers with your child and have them speak to people who actually do the work. I find it very strange how some teenagers come to a conclusion on what they "would like to do when they grow up." If you have a teenager in your life you may be able to appreciate, if not always understand, the thought processes they employ. The best way to shed some light on their thinking is to discuss these topics with them. It should always be in a positive way, even if they claim to want to be the next famous athlete or rock star. None of this is easy as this is may be an age where your child does not particularly want to talk to you about anything. This is where your earlier discussions, when your child was younger but possibly more agreeable, really make a big difference in ensuring they don't get too far off the track.

This is also a good age to discuss college with your child. This will be covered in greater detail later. Whether your child is certain he wants to go to college, is uncertain or is downright sure he does not want to go to college, you should discuss it. A college degree has been shown to greatly increase one's lifetime earnings. With that said, college is not the answer for every child. However, further education is the answer for everyone in obtaining a better financial life. Whether it is an Associates Degree or a Technical Certification, greater education, on average, pays off in the long run.

Children who are very eager to earn money right out of high school usually hurt their chances for greater wealth down the road. Yes, if you start working at 18 instead of 22, you'll have more money sooner, but in almost all cases, a post high school degree will ensure greater earnings over your child's lifetime. There is plenty of research on the topic that may be found on the internet.

No matter what line of work or career your child decides on the aim of the game is to earn as much as possible on your chosen path. The more your child earns, the more he or she is likely to save and this will have a direct effect on their future wealth.

I have seen both extremes as families encourage their children in a particular direction when it comes to a career. The first extreme is to tell children that money does not matter and that they should do something that they love. I completely agree that working at something you love is one of the most important goals in life. However, thinking that money is not part of the equation in working is to be naïve. Our society requires money and if you have no money, or very little, life can be very hard and quite frustrating. I suggest that you discuss the monetary aspect of any career with your children. They should know by the time they are in their teens that things in life cost money. To be comfortable and enjoy at least some of life's simple pleasures requires some level of financial wherewithal. Your child should learn that earning money is a part of the satisfaction of working. Working hard and then staring down at a very small paycheck is not at all satisfying. I know because I have done it. I have many peers who wish they had taken money more seriously when they were considering a career.

The other extreme is to make money the most important aspect of working. This is a big mistake. Yes, we all know money is important and if your child is headed to a career, of their own choosing, with substantial financial benefits, then you may have one less worry in life. But, I do not condone pushing any child down a career path solely because of the financial gain to be had. There are too many stories of people waking up in their thirties and forties to find they work at something they first tolerated and now hate simply because the pay was good. Realizing this at forty five will truly put things into perspective. Again, balance is the important consideration. Balancing the financial aspect of a particular career with the other, intangible benefits and with what your child loves to do will be the best course of action.

     Earning a salary, unfortunately, is only the first hurdle that your child must face as he or she strives for financial freedom and wealth. Why is it that there are far more people with high incomes than there are wealthy people?

Pillar Two: Save

While income is an important determinate to financial well being, at the end of the day, it matters most how much one saves from this income. There are people, some of them famous athletes and movie stars, who earn millions of dollars a year and still wind up broke and sometimes bankrupt. Most people think it is impossible to earn that kind of money and go bankrupt. Obviously, this is not the case. Apparently, it is all too easy to do. There are three reasons why.

One very common cause of poor financial health is overspending. Whether you earn $10,000 a year or $10 million a year if you spend more than you earn, you will go backwards financially. If you earn $10,000 a year after taxes and spend $10,001 a year you will be in worse financial shape one year from now than you are today. The same holds true if you spend one dollar more than your $10 million yearly income.

Our country is a great country in more ways than one. It is a land of opportunity and the financial possibilities are almost limitless. It is also a country where no matter how high your income it is usually possible to spend more than you earn. This problem is far too common. It happens to people with high incomes, average incomes and low incomes. If you cannot save something when you have an income then you will never make progress.

I have several friends who are financial planners and they can go on and on about some of their clients with high incomes who have retained very little of what they earn and hence have no appreciable wealth. They also have plenty of stories about average people with average incomes who have saved and invested wisely and as a result have a considerable level of wealth.

The savings plan that we will cover below is designed to create permanent savings. This is savings that should never be touched as it will be used to build wealth down the road. Many people are very good at saving intensely for short periods of time. They then take this savings and spend it all on things like boats, TVs, VCRs, clothes and furniture. While there is nothing wrong with this approach, it achieves the same result as not saving day in and day out. That result is that there are no savings! The goal with permanent savings is that it is not touched to buy depreciating assets (we'll cover this later). These are things that go down in value after we buy them. The only thing that your child will "spend" his or her permanent savings on will be investments.

The rule that you should introduce your children to as they earn money is the Rule of Saving First. The Rule of Saving First is so simple yet so powerful that once your child has practiced and taken this rule to heart, he or she will be well on the way to making significant financial progress in the years to come. The Rule of Saving First is the only way to approach a savings program. Most people approach saving in the following way:

<u>Common Approach to Saving</u>

Income – Taxes – Required Expenses – Other Expenses = Savings

The mistake that most people make is that they have the order wrong. The Rule of Saving First approaches saving in the following manner:

<u>The Rule of Saving First Approach to Saving</u>

Income – Taxes – <u>Savings</u> = Required Expenses + Other Expenses

The Rule of Saving First will ensure that your child always pays himself first before paying anyone else. This is not to say that you should teach your child not pay his bills or to become a deadbeat. What the Rule of Saving First ensures is that your child will pay himself first and then live within his means by confining his expenditures to what is leftover. It seems so simple and so obvious, but it is clearly against human nature to pay oneself first. Just as we have to learn to be polite and learn good table manners, saving money does not seem to come naturally to most people. There are countries that save a significant portion of their incomes, but America is not one of these.

Since both the Common Approach to Saving and the Rule of Saving First require paying taxes and required expenses, obviously the largest difference, assuming the Rule of Saving First saver saves more, is in how much each saver spends on Other Expenses. As we will see shortly, the Wealthy Child will save more and therefore have less to spend on Other Expenses.

How is it that by simply changing the order of terms in the saving formula your child will save more money? The answer is that two critical components must follow the Rule of Saving First. The first component is the Rule of 10 to 100 and the second is the Rule of No Credit.

The Rule of 10 to 100 states that your child should always save somewhere between 10% and 100% of their income. This is the breakdown:

Ages 0 through 5: A child, or you on their behalf, should save nearly 100% of their income. Their income is primarily from gifts from friends and family. Birthday money, money obtained from religious events and the like should be saved entirely. You are paying the expenses related to your child's clothing, food and housing and he or she should save just about everything they "earn." This money, although most likely small in total amount, will have decades to grow and can have a huge impact on your child's future financial well being. Did you know that $20, left to compound for 65 years (typical retirement age) at 10% annually (ignoring taxes) will grow to $176,613!

Ages 5 through 17: This is a broad age range, but it is also a period of your child's life where he will learn a great deal of the habits that follow him for the rest of his life. During this period of time, your child should save 50% of every dollar he earns. You will still be supporting your child and most of the expenses he has will be discretionary. 50% is certainly an impressive goal, but it will help them later in life as this money is invested. Furthermore, 50%, or half, is an easy figure to calculate for any sum of money. Get your children into the saving habit by having them save half of everything they earn during this period of their lives.

When your child becomes a teenager and is able to legally work in your state consider a part time job for him or her. There are different schools of thought on this issue. Many families feel that part time jobs are not important and that school and school activities should come first. Yes, your child's primary mission is to become educated and take full advantage of his schooling. This will help him tremendously in the future. However, a part time job is crucial to your child's understanding of the value of money. Too many parents have their children focus on schooling and simply hand the children money when they need it. This teaches the wrong lesson. Your child needs to learn that money is to be earned. If you can, match their earnings and have them contribute this money to a Roth IRA (covered later).

Ages 17 through 21: This is a tough age range because many young people are either heading off to college or entering the workforce. The rule here is to save as much as possible, but always at least 10%. During your child's late teens and early twenties they will form many opinions and ways of thinking that will be with them for the rest of the lives. If you look back at your own life you will see that this is usually the case. Make sure that your child stays on the path that you and he have followed so far. If he continues to live and master the basics of personal finance there is a very good chance that he will be a financial success going forward.

Ages 21 through 30: While your child may be heading off to get an advanced degree after college, many young people are firmly entrenched in the workforce during this period of time and getting their footing in "the real world." During this period while they are employed, your child should save 20% of her salary with no exceptions. As hard as your daughter may think it is to save 20% of her salary, I can assure you that it will be harder for her to do so in the future. Plus, if she wants money for a down payment on a home in the years to come, saving now is an absolute must. Many young people fail to save because they cannot envision their financial needs in 5 to 10 years. A young person may think that he doesn't really need or want a house. He may think that retirement, 30 to 50 years into the future, is unimportant or that there will be "enough time later" to save. All too often these financial "needs" creep up too quickly and a child wishes he had saved more money earlier.

As your child may now have access to a retirement plan, such as a 401(k) and/or an IRA, keep in mind that the 20% savings target includes all savings and that encompasses retirement accounts.

Ages 30 and beyond: As your child grows older, he may buy a home, get married and have children. While these events are not part of everyone's life one thing is for certain. As we grow older our financial responsibilities seem to grow as well. The target during this long stretch of life is to save as much as possible, but never less than 10%. This can be a difficult task at times, but the payoff down the road is certainly worth it.

Many people ask how they should calculate their current savings rate. Divide the amount saved in the last year by the salary during the year. Let's take the example of someone earning $50,000 a year and saving $7,800 a year:

$7,800 / $50,000 = .1560 or 15.60%

To determine how much they should save, take the desired savings rates and multiply by the annual salary. Let's say that your child is 23 years old and agrees that he should be saving 20% of his $25,000 salary as outlined above:

.20 x $25,000 = $5,000

The Rule of No Credit

Your child may be saving a good portion of her income. From a cash flow point of view everything may look rosy. But, there are many, many ways to make financial mistakes and to be hurt by making poor decisions. Debt and credit can be good or bad depending on how they are used. Even if your child is saving but accumulating debt, especially if it is not against an appreciating asset then she may be headed for trouble in the future.

There are plenty of credit cards, mortgages and home loans that offer a very low introductory interest rate that increases at some time in the future. That increasing rate may allow your child to save money today but be unable to do so in the future as the amount of money needed to pay interest on that debt increases. That is why saving money alone is not always enough to reach one's financial goals.

The second component that must go with the Rule of Saving First is the Rule of No Credit. You should instill in your child the notion that she should never, ever buy typical, everyday items on credit or by using a credit card. Some of life's major purchases will require buying with a loan or on credit. However, clothes, food, electronics and other consumer goods should never be bought on credit. Some of the most unhappy young people today are those who are struggling under a mountain of credit card debt that they may never be able to get out from under. These are typically the people who, in their thirties, are paying off the pizza they ate in their twenties. They may be paying off credit card debt at the same time they are paying off college and possibly graduate school loans. This invariably is occurring at the same time the child is looking to buy a home but has no hope of saving enough for a down payment as he has to continuously pay interest on these other loans and credit cards.

We will talk about credit cards in detail later. Right now, let's go through a brief discussion while we are talking about the Rule of No Credit. Credit cards have caused more financial difficulty for the average American than anything else. Most people find the notion of spending what they do not have simply irresistible. They spend today and only worry about the consequences later. There are always stories in the popular press and financial publications about young people, who have low incomes and tremendous amounts of credit card debt, who can only make the minimum payment on their credit card bills. In some cases, these young people will be paying these bills for decades to come and will have paid many, many times the original amount borrowed over that time.

Many young people feel that if their debt becomes too great they will simply declare bankruptcy and walk away from their obligations. There is no longer the social stigma associated with bankruptcy that there used to be for previous generations. Well, the law changed not too long ago and it is now much harder to declare bankruptcy. It is not an option for most people. The best way to steer clear of the "debt problem" is to have a plan from the start and make responsible decisions along the way.

Teach your child that all expenses should be paid out of current income and that purchases of clothes, food and other small items should be paid for by cash or by check. Your child will need at least one credit card for many reasons. The most important reason is that a credit card can be very useful in an emergency if your child needs fast access to quick cash. If your child puts this credit card, or two cards, in her purse in a small sealed envelope marked EMERGENCY, this will be a constant reminder of the credit card's purpose. If your child has more credit cards that should be kept for the long haul but not used for purchases or for emergencies she may freeze these in a block of ice in the freezer. This way the card may be used if needed by thawing the ice out but it is unlikely that an impulse purchase will be made using this credit card.

The statements from this credit card should be sent to you, the parent, and not the child. The statement may be in your daughter's name, but it should be mailed to your address so that you can constantly monitor expenditures. This is especially true during the college years. Even responsible children seem to have a tendency to spend too freely on credit cards when they get to college.

Many credit cards have tempting offers that we all see for 0% loans and credit card offers. Don't let your child fall for the 0% trap. Many credit card companies and stores offer 0% loans if you buy their products. If your child does not have the money then she should not buy the item even if the interest rate offered is 0%. The 0% always looks attractive to people, but even if the interest rate is 0% your child will still need to pay the principal back. Usually what happens to borrowers of these 0% interest rate loans is that they can't pay the principal back fast enough to meet the loan agreement and the interest rate then jumps to something around 20%! The companies that offer these 0% loans are not entirely stupid. They know that a good number of their customers will fall into this trap and wind up paying a much higher rate for years to come.

Many young people are using these 0% offers, taking money from their credit card and then investing that money at a bank and receiving the interest. This is an economically rational endeavor but your child should be careful because if they make one late payment or get tripped up by some other part of the credit card agreement then the economics completely fall apart and it will wind up costing money.

Teach your son or daughter to save for the things they want. This is above and beyond the savings we discussed above that will go to her Savings Box. She will use the other 50% of her income for the things that she wants to buy. As we will see later, a savings account at a local bank will be a good place for this money and will get your child familiar with the concept of savings and saving her money at a bank.

The Savings Box

     The Savings Box is a great idea for children and will really help them learn the concept of saving. You should start a Savings Box with your child when he or she is ready. This is usually around the age of five. Your child should have some idea about money and how to count it. He should know the difference between all of the coins and the bills. He should be able to figure, sometimes with your help, what 50%, or half, of any amount of money is. This will be the amount that he saves from all of his income for the next twelve years from the age of 5 through the age of 17.
     The critical lesson that your child should learn from using the Savings Box is that this money will be saved for a very, very long period of time and maybe forever! This is not money that your child will save to buy a toy. He will do this with the other 50% of his income. The money he saves in his Savings Box will be put to work and will grow on its own into a larger amount in the future through investing and the power of compounding. The money that he is putting away will be used for two critically important goals:

- To build his wealth

- To provide financial security

Half of everything your child earns or receives will be used for only these two goals. The money in the Savings Box will build his wealth over time. This money will grow to a substantial sum over time if your young child continues to save and invest a portion of his income in the decades to come. This money will provide tremendous financial security and peace of mind. This intangible benefit will be worth its weight in gold for your child in the decades to come as it will help lessen his financial worries.

The Savings Box may be something as simple as a cardboard box that will allow your child to put money in but not take it out. It may be a lockbox, where you keep the key and your child can place money in through a slit at the top. It may be the old style piggy bank as well. While it really does not matter what type of "box" you and your child use to save his money it is a good idea to have your child be part of building his own Savings Box. If your child is very involved in the process, starting with building his own Savings Box, he is more likely to follow through with the entire program because the Savings Box is something he built or helped build and he is involved and has invested his time into this program.

He will not, and should not be able, to get this money. This is one of the critical aspects of your child saving half of all money he receives and placing it in the Savings Box. This money, theoretically, is never to be spent. It should be left to grow. It may even be used, or partially used, to help your child's children or maybe even his grandchildren. Make sure that your child understands this. The money in the Savings Box is not to be touched and is to be left to grow. Your child will save some of the other half of the money he receives which is that half that does not go into the Savings Box. He must learn to live on and spend for "fun" out of the money that is leftover after he has paid himself first.

You will be gatekeeper and should have access to the money as you will want to invest it (we'll cover this later) once the amount he saves reaches something in the $50 to $100 range. When you and your child remove money to have it invested somewhere make sure that you write on a slip of paper the amount of the money that was removed, the date and where and how the money was invested. Place this slip of paper into your child's Savings Box.

Money being whisked off to a mutual fund or an Exchange Traded Fund (ETF) (see Appendix G for more on ETFs) is something that is too abstract for most young children. They will need the slip of paper as a physical reminder that they have a sum of money invested somewhere and that the total amount of money that they have invested has been growing over time. These slips of paper, along with your child's log, will show him that his wealth is growing. By making sure that he performs these administrative tasks when needed you will be teaching him to be organized and precise about his money and to know exactly how much money he has and where that money resides. Financial precision was discussed briefly under Pillar One and will be covered again in detail later in the book. Applying financial precision to all of his money flows is an important skill that will benefit your child later in life.

The Age Old Battle: Needs vs. Wants

It was wisely stated a long time ago that "health is the greatest happiness and contentment the greatest wealth." Being content with what one has is very difficult and takes a lot of practice. Another astute observer said, "There are two ways to be rich. Earn more or want less." Keeping our spending in check is much easier than working to earn additional money.

One of the best ways you can help your child save is by making sure they understand themselves, human nature and needs versus wants. Understanding the difference between the two is critical. Saving money and eventually building wealth is a constant struggle that will require sacrifices from your child. These sacrifices will be many at times, but one sacrifice that all wealth builders must make is that of saving. In order to save your child must spend less than she earns. For this to happen, your child must not spend all of the money she earns. In order for this to happen your child must adhere to two rules:

Keep required expenses reasonable in relation to income. There are no set figures or percentages for what constitutes reasonable, but if your child aims to save and their required expenses leave them with practically nothing at the end of the month, saving will be almost impossible and your child will have no "fun money" for other expenses such as a dinner out or a movie or a new laptop.

Other Expenses must be kept to a reasonable level. Again, there is no ratio or figure that is set in stone for other expenses. However, if one's other expenses grow closer to 10% of one's pre-tax income, this seems high to me. Again, it depends on one's income. If your income is high enough and you save 40% of it while still spending 15% of it on other expenses, this is probably fine. Most of us are not this lucky to have so much room in our budgets.

You should spend a lot of time with your child so that she understands the difference between needs and wants. This is a hard lesson for children to learn as they are quick to decide and usually want most everything they see. They should learn to think through their purchase and if they will actually use and enjoy what they are considering buying. Much of consumerism, and advertising, is focused on the process of consuming and buying rather than the good use of the items purchased and those that we own already. It is important that your children learn this.

A big part of distinguishing between needs and wants is being able to decide on the value of an item to one's self. When I was a freshman in college I paid the princely sum of $700 for a road bicycle. It was a large part of the money I had at the time. Some financial gurus would say that this was a completely unnecessary expense. In many ways it was as I certainly did not need a bicycle in the same sense that I needed food or needed a place to live. I didn't even need the bicycle to get somewhere on a regular basis.

But, I used that bicycle religiously over the next 8 years and put many thousands of miles on it while getting into shape. The bicycle had tremendous value to me. If I had bought it and left it in the basement it would have been not only an unnecessary expense, it would have been a complete waste of money. But, I realized so much enjoyment from that bicycle, spent so much time using and got into shape. That made the purchase worthwhile. Remember the old axiom, "The fool knows the price of everything and the value of nothing."

Exercise Discipline and Delay Gratification

In order to control the amount of money your child spends on other expenses, she will need to deny herself from time to time. This requires a sense of purpose of saving and growing wealth. Almost everyone wants to save money and grow their wealth. It is rare that you meet someone who does not want these things. But, like most of what people want in life, it comes to nothing without a program, a goal and discipline. The best way to build discipline in this area is to exercise your "financial discipline muscle."

Discipline works very much like a muscle in your arm or leg. The more you use the muscle, the stronger it gets. The best way to exercise financial discipline is to start small. It is possible to strain or tear a muscle by trying to put it through a regimen that it is not prepared for. The same is true of your child's financial discipline muscle. Small, progressive steps over a period months and years works best to build this muscle. Your child should start out by denying themselves small things that they seem to want only for the sake of wanting them. As your child builds his discipline, your child will be able to deny himself things that he actually does want!

Young children must learn financial discipline, to delay gratification and to save for the future. For your child to realize these goals she will need to be able to compare two choices, spending now or saving for the future, and compare the benefits of having something now for her money versus saving the money, investing it and have it grow for the future. Most young children have neither the mental capability nor the experience to follow this thought process and this is OK. If you continue to go through this exercise with your child she will be familiar with the thought process and at some point will be ready to make her own decisions.

Don't let your child try to go from living it up and blowing all of her money to trying to live like pauper. This will not work anymore than trying to force a couch potato to finish a marathon tomorrow with decent results. If your child is a spender you'll need to have her realize for herself that saving is an important and fun goal. If she agrees with the goal, denying herself will be much, much easier. The transition will work best if you and your child make small steps over long periods of time. This will build a strong foundation and allow her to gradually change her behavior for the better. Keep in mind that our children do as we do and not as we say. One of the best ways to instill any type of behavior in your child is to follow that behavior in your own life for your child to see day in and day out.

This will be a hard road for you and your child as the American society doesn't really work this way. Your child's friends will probably spend money without any concept of the money's value. The American culture is a strange miasma of notions, beliefs and hopes. Americans seem to think, or at least hope, that the future will be better, brighter and rosier than today because we certainly, as a country, are not saving for a rainy day. Our government cannot even control its own spending. These are the forces that you will fight on a daily basis as you teach your child the right way to think about money and personal finance. Your child will constantly be exposed to main categories of persuasive motivation:

What she sees around her in her everyday life

Advertising

      Your child will go through her daily life and inadvertently pick up many ideas and notions about life. She will see the kind of houses people live in. She will see the cars that they drive. She will hear about the vacations people take. She will see the toys that other children receive for special occasions or maybe for no particular reason at all. She may see some other children receive cars when they turn 16 years old. All of this information is taken in by your child and not always filtered by reason. It simply in her mind becomes "the way things are." This is tremendous and constant societal pressure that drives behavior and can shape your child's behavior in the years to come.

      Advertising is another powerful force in your child's life. When she watches TV or goes to a restaurant she will be exposed to advertising. When you and your child are in the supermarket she will be exposed to advertising. When she is on the internet she will be exposed to advertising. Advertising is everywhere and there is no way to escape it except to change your child's thinking about the world around her and advertising.

Your child should know that your family has rules. Some of the rules concern keeping the house clean and each family member sharing in tasks such as emptying the garbage and cleaning up common spaces. Other rules are a little harder for young children to understand but they should be taught that your family's rules are for your family and may be different from other families' rules. She should learn that it doesn't matter if Tommy was given a particular toy or if Cindy can spend all of her money. Your family has rules that work and everyone should stick to them. Over time you'll be able to show your child why your family's rules do work and this is particularly applicable in the case of financial rules.

The Power of Advertising

Teach your children how powerful advertising can be. There have been many studies performed that show how children of various ages are affected by advertising. The studies have shown that young children often times have trouble discriminating between reality and fantasy and that they are very impressionable.

Trying to discuss the mechanics of advertising and the power it can have over them is pointless. It won't be until the age of 7 or 8 that you will be able to discuss logically with your child the tremendous power advertising can have in making us want things that we do not really need.

The best way to teach children younger than this that they cannot have everything that they see is to teach them as quickly as possible about money, saving their money and then have them decide how to spend their money. There will be times that your child will be able to ask for a particular toy or toys and he should receive at least some of what he asks for. There are occasions for this, such as birthdays and other celebrations.

However, day in and day out you should not buy a toy just because your child asks for it. Your child should learn to use his own money to buy these toys. It is fine if you decide to share the cost with him of a certain toy but he must learn that he cannot have everything he sees for many reasons. The most important of all the reasons is that <u>resources are limited and money is a limited resource</u>. Your child will have to make decisions as to how he will spend his money. He will have to make the hard choices that must be made through every stage of life. While there will certainly be temper tantrums and complaining about this policy, slowly your child will learn to budget and choose how to spend his money. This one lesson will give your child a huge advantage later in life.

For older children, you may discuss what advertising is and how it works. Advertising's aim is to stimulate demand. Hopefully, your child is slowly learning the difference between needs and wants. Advertising strives to put images and scenarios in your child's mind as to the benefits of a particular toy or game. You should work with your child when they come to you stating that they want a particular toy. You should discuss with them why they want that toy and why they think they should have that toy.

Track, Track, Track Your Expenses

This part of Pillar Two really is not fun. It requires your child to track his or her expenses every week throughout the entire year. This routine applies financial precision to expenses and is lacking in most people's financial plans.

If your child does not know how much he is spending, by category, he will have no idea at the end of the year if he is happy with his level of spending in each category. As your child becomes a young adult, tracking his expenses will be especially important because his life will be more complicated and he will have more expenses than he will be able to remember.

By keeping a log of these expenses, he will know how much he is spending on utilities, eating out, eating in, traveling and other categories. At the end of year, after tracking his expenses, he may decide to make no changes to his spending patterns or he may be surprised how much he spends on a particular category and decide to cut back in the year that follows. Since his savings rate will be greatly affected by his expenses, he will have more knowledge of his spending patterns and therefore more control to affect change should he decide to do so.

One of the best ways to track expenses is to keep a small notebook at home and every time your child spends money, he or she should enter the amount and the reason for the expenditure in this notebook. Most people don't track their expenses at all and therefore have absolutely no idea where their money goes and no idea why they don't have any money left at the end of the month and cannot save. In fact, you'll often times hear people say, "I have no idea where the money goes!" If you don't track your money, you will not have any idea where it goes unless your financial life is very, very simple.

When people, who historically have not tracked their expenses, begin to do so, they are usually shocked at the total amount of money they spend on unneeded expenses. They are also shocked at the amount of money spent on particular categories, such as food or drinks. This is usually what motivates people to begin saving.

Your child should track his expenses religiously. Since he is not using a credit card for anything other than emergencies and large, pre-planned purchases, he will be paying for other expenses with cash. This cash will be a preset amount that he has decided on in advance for the week. If he reaches Thursday and has no money then he should spend no more until Monday. Even with this fail safe mechanism of using only cash in place, your child will learn a lot about how he spends money and how he may save money in the future by tracking his expenses.

I had a friend who had worked hard for many years and was doing very well in business. I had known him since we were both children. When we were in the eighth grade he caught the car bug. He couldn't wait until he was old enough to get his license. He knew the make, model and year of every car that drove by. He learned about engines, tires, transmissions and brakes. He swore that one day he would go out and buy a Porsche. It was his obsession all through high school and college. Every time a Porsche drove by his jaw dropped to the ground.

I caught up with him about ten years after we had graduated college. It was obvious that he was doing well financially and as we sat and talked over lunch it became clear that we agreed on many points about earning, saving and investing money. If anything, he was far more frugal than I. Finally, I had to ask him if he ever went out and bought a Porsche. Since he was not one to boast about his money, he blushed and replied, "You know I always wanted a Porsche. For as long as I can remember I wanted to buy that car. I continued to want a

Porsche right up until the point where I could afford one and then a funny thing happened. Knowing that I could afford it, I no longer really wanted it. I decided that I would rather have the money and have it add to my wealth in the future. Oh, but I did rent the fastest Porsche they make for one day. This got 'wanting one' entirely out of my system."

My friend had clearly understood the difference between a need a want. He did not need a Porsche, but he did desperately want one. He also had spent the last decade tracking his expenses. As he was keenly aware of the costs to buy and maintain such a car, he could not justify the expense of a brand new Porsche.

Pillar Three: Time to Invest and Grow

While earning an income and saving a good portion of that income will be critical to your child's financial health and success your child will also need to master the skills required to grow his savings over time. There are two components to investing money and have it grow. The first is time. Generally, the longer a sum of money is invested the greater the amount of that sum at the end of the time period. The second component is the interest rate at which money will grow. A positive interest rate, growing over time exhibits a phenomenon seen in the natural world known as compounding.

Nothing But Time

When Albert Einstein was asked what the greatest force in the universe was many expected his answer to "a black hole," or maybe "the sun," but instead he said "compounding."

Another great thinker, Benjamin Franklin, was so adept at business and financial matters that he had earned a fortune before he was thirty years old. He is said to have coined the phrase, "a penny saved is a penny earned."

Ben Franklin was so enamored with the concept of compounding that when he died in 1790 his will stipulated that 1,000 pounds each be left to the cities of Boston and Philadelphia. Each city was to invest the money at 5% and leave it untouched for 100 years. At the end of 100 years the city was allowed to spend three quarters of the balance on projects to improve the city. The rest was to be invested for another 100 years.

To simplify the example somewhat, after 200 years the original investment, had it been untouched, would have been worth over 17 million pounds or about $32 million using a 2007 exchange rate!

Now, most people are not very interested in investing for 200 years so let us look at some more realistic and shorter term examples.

Below, is a table that shows the growth of $1 at the stated interest rate over a specified period of time (years). For example, $1 invested at 6% over 10 years will yield $1.79 (shown in bold below). If you had invested $40 instead of $1 you can figure out the amount by multiplying $40 by 1.79 or $71.60. Your child should become familiar with this chart to understand the true power of compounding.

Years

Rate	1	2	4	6	8	10	12	14
2%	$1.02	$1.04	$1.08	$1.13	$1.17	$1.22	$1.27	$1.32
4%	$1.04	$1.08	$1.17	$1.27	$1.37	$1.48	$1.60	$1.73
6%	$1.06	$1.12	$1.26	$1.42	$1.59	**$1.79**	$2.01	$2.26
8%	$1.08	$1.17	$1.36	$1.59	$1.85	$2.16	$2.52	$2.94
10%	$1.10	$1.21	$1.46	$1.77	$2.14	$2.59	$3.14	$3.80
12%	$1.12	$1.25	$1.57	$1.97	$2.48	$3.11	$3.90	$4.89
14%	$1.14	$1.30	$1.69	$2.19	$2.85	$3.71	$4.82	$6.26
16%	$1.16	$1.35	$1.81	$2.44	$3.28	$4.41	$5.94	$7.99
18%	$1.18	$1.39	$1.94	$2.70	$3.76	$5.23	$7.29	$10.15
20%	$1.20	$1.44	$2.07	$2.99	$4.30	$6.19	$8.92	$12.84
22%	$1.22	$1.49	$2.22	$3.30	$4.91	$7.30	$10.87	$16.18
24%	$1.24	$1.54	$2.36	$3.64	$5.59	$8.59	$13.21	$20.32
26%	$1.26	$1.59	$2.52	$4.00	$6.35	$10.09	$16.01	$25.42
28%	$1.28	$1.64	$2.68	$4.40	$7.21	$11.81	$19.34	$31.69
30%	$1.30	$1.69	$2.86	$4.83	$8.16	$13.79	$23.30	$39.37

A few things become apparent in the chart above. The first is that time makes a big difference in the growth of any amount of money invested today. We saw how $40 would grow to $71.60 in 10 years at an interest rate of 6%. Look at what happens when that same $40 is invested for 20 years at 6% rate of interest. It grows to $128.29!

The other very obvious factor at work is the rate of interest. If that $40 had been invested at 10% instead of 6% for 20 years the resulting sum would be $269.10 or 2.09 times more than the $128.29 realized at a 6% rate of interest.

It is very important that your child understand the math behind compounding. Since the calculation is difficult for long periods of time your child will need to use a calculator or an Excel worksheet. Remember, a very large percentage of the population does not understand the mathematics behind compound interest and your child should know how to calculate the resulting sum if the period and rate of interest are given. I know that most of us are not fond of formulas, but here it is:

$(1+ \text{Interest Rate in Decimal Form})^{\text{Years}}$

This is a very simple formula that states that you take the interest rate, say 6%, in decimal form, or .06, add 1 to it, obtaining 1.06 and then raise this amount to the power of 20. In this case Years = 20 because we invest the money for 20 years. If you know the rate of interest simply divide it by 100 to obtain the decimal form. So, 6 divided by 100 is .06.

Your child may use a calculator and check the results in the table above. Let's take a look at the table above where $1 is invested at 16% for 4 years. The calculation is as follows:

Time invested = 4 years

Interest Rate = 16% divided by 100 = .16

$(1+.16)^4 = \$1.81$

Some calculators depict "to the power of" as y^x and in Excel you must use ^ and the formula is (1 +.16)^4. It is critical that your child learn to calculate the growth of money using this formula. Do not assume that they will learn this in school. In fact, depending on your child's course of study she may not come across this concept until she is in college or graduate school.

The Penny Game

As your child learns about money he or she will also need to learn about various forms of money. There are coins and there are bills. As they begin to grasp these concepts you should introduce them to the power of compounding by playing The Penny Game. Children are old enough for this game when they understand the difference between a penny, a nickel, a dime, a quarter and a dollar bill. Also, they ideally should have some concept about what the things they like cost.

The Penny Game is very simple. You begin with a large jar of pennies. On the first day, you place one penny on a table and explain to your child that each day the number of pennies will double. This is compounding. You will play the game for two weeks.

Week One:

On Monday, there is 1 penny on the table.

On Tuesday, there are 2 pennies on the table.

On Wednesday, there are 4 pennies on the table.

On Thursday, there are 8 pennies on the table.

On Friday, there are 16 pennies on the table.

On Saturday, there are 32 pennies on the table.

On Sunday, there are 64 pennies on the table.

     At the end of week one, 1 penny has grown to 64 pennies or 64 cents. This is not at all spectacular, but that 1 penny has come a long way. It is at this time, that you should start using dollar bills going into the next week!

Week Two:

On Monday, there are 128 pennies or $1.28, which is 1 dollar bill and 28 pennies.

On Tuesday, there are 256 pennies or $2.56, which is 2 dollar bills and 56 pennies.

On Wednesday, there are 512 pennies or $5.12 which is 5 dollar bills and 12 pennies.

On Thursday, there are 1,024 pennies or $10.24, which is 10 dollar bills and 24 pennies.

On Friday, there are 2,048 pennies or $20.48, which is 20 dollar bills and 48 pennies.

On Saturday, there are 4,096 pennies or $40.96, which is 40 dollar bills and 96 pennies.

On Sunday, there are 8,192 pennies or $81.92, which is 81 dollars and 92 pennies.

After two weeks, that 1 penny has grown to $81.92. Discuss with your child that this is what happens when you invest your money and it grows by compounding. They should be rather impressed when they see what can be bought with $81.92!

If your children are older and not impressed with $81.92, you may need to move up to The Nickel Game in Appendix A. Save your dollar bills for this game because at the end of two weeks The Nickel Game yields $409.60!

A Good Example for Your Child

The following example has been very popular within the financial planning community for many years now and there is good reason. This example shows the power of compounding and starting early.

In this example there are twins, Tom and Dave. Tom has always been a go getter and likes to start things early. Dave has always been a procrastinator and not for any particularly good reason. Tom and Dave both go to work for the same company, XYZ, Inc. at the age of 22. Tom immediately enrolls in the company's 401(k) plan and begins contributing $100 a month to the 401(k) plan. At the age of 42, after 20 years of contributing to the 401(k) plan, Tom decides to retire from XYZ, Inc., stops contributing to the 401(k) plan and travels around the world helping poor people build homes.

Dave waits until he and his brother are 35 years old to contribute to the 401(k) plan and decides to invest $100 a month from his paycheck as well. Dave contributes to the plan for 20 years as well and stops when he turns 55 years old.

Both brothers realize an annualized 7% return in their 401(k) plans each year. At the age of 65, Dave has $99,841 in his 401(k) plan. Tom has $240,599 or $140,758 more than Dave. This is truly a staggering difference in the result even though each brother contributed exactly $24,000 to the 401(k) plan over 20 years. When it comes to investing the sooner money is put to work the better.

How to Invest for Your Child Early

While we are on the subject of compounding, we should take a moment to cover the topic of investing for your children. While specific investments and vehicles will be covered later in the book, the concept of investing and investing early is a critical one.

Whether your child is a newborn or fifteen years old, he has time on his side and compounding is all about time. The more time the child has ahead of him, the better. As a parent, don't confine your thinking of time to the period from today until your child is 21 years old. Think across their entire expected lifespan. Someone born today or within the last 10 years has a very, very good chance of living to be 80, 90 or even older. Think in terms of the future value of each dollar you invest today for your child. This is a much wider topic than just helping them save for college or for their first car. Remember, small amounts of money invested over long periods of time become very large sums of money. Not only would your child have that money and the security that comes with it, she would also hopefully always remember that someone in her life was really looking out for her and put this money away for her future.

Let's say that you saved $2 a day, every day for your child from the time she was born until she was 18 years old. At the end of each year you took that money and invested it at a 10% rate of return. At the end of her 20th year, your child would have $35,813.14. If this money stayed invested for another 10 years, at the age of 30 she would have almost $93,000. If the money was invested for another 10 years, at the age of 40 she would have nearly $241,000. If this money continued to be invested until she was 65 years old, or another 25 years, your daughter would have over $2.6 million. All from only saving $2 a day for the first 18 years of her life. Always think of the long term compounding effect of money. Think of how much money your child would have when he reaches your current age. Think of how your life would be changed if someone had invested for you at an early age and that money had been untouched and left to compound. Most of us would have far fewer financial worries if this had been the case.

The true power of compounding is that small sums of money invested over long periods of time grow to substantial amounts. Don't fall into the trap of thinking that you need a certain amount of money for your child before you can invest. It is much better to start small and early than it is to start big and late (or never).

There are many different ways to invest money for your child so that it will grow over time. Here are some of the options:

- Savings or Money Market Account
- Checking Account
- 529 College Savings Plan
- Uniform Transfer to Minors Act also known as a UTMA (we'll talk about this later) and Uniform Gift to Minor's Act (UGMA)

Savings Money Market and Checking Accounts

While your child should hold some money in a savings account or a money market account at his local bank the low returns on such accounts dictate that your child invest in higher yielding investments. However, it is good practice for him to deposit money from time and also to withdraw it from time to time. Another benefit of your child having an account is that if you ever need to move money into one of your child's other investment accounts, say a UTMA, it will be easy. You'll simply have a money order or a bank check drawn against your child's account and made payable so that it may be deposited in another account. Your young child likely does not need a checkbook and the additional administrative work is not worth it at a young age. As he gets older he will need a checkbook to meet expenses and keeping track of a checkbook is a good exercise for him.

529 College Savings Plans

After the goal of saving for your retirement your next biggest financial challenge is probably saving for your child's education. If you have small children and are not yet aware of the future expected cost of college then you'll need to understand the expected cost so that you may plan. Conservative estimates now place the cost of four years at a public university (usually cheaper than a private university) at $100,000 or more in 15 years. There are many calculators on the internet that will allow you examine your own situation and savings plans and change some assumptions to fit your particular goal.

If you have recovered from either already knowing the cost of a college education for your child or you are just getting a taste, keep in mind that many of today's children will go on to receive a graduate degree after graduating college!

529 College Savings are a fantastic way to save for your child's future education expenses. Most financial planners feel that 529 College Savings Plans are now the best way to save for a child's higher education expenses but speak to your own financial advisor to

determine which route is best for you as we will not cover other options such as the Coverdell plan or prepaid tuition plans.

529 plans are state sponsored and the options, rules and restrictions vary by state. The state sets up the plan with an asset management company such as Vanguard, Fidelity or another similar institution. You are not confined to investing in your state's plan. You may invest in any state's plan if you feel that it suits your needs. However, you usually will receive some form of state income tax deduction if you contribute to your state's plan rather than a plan from another state.

While plans differ by state, and you will need to check the details for your plan, we should begin by dismissing some of the common myths surrounding 529 plans.

- A child must go to college in the state where his or her 529 plan is held. This is false. Your child may go to any school in any state. The 529 plan is for higher education expenses and is not restricted to any school or state.

- A child must go to a state school if they use the proceeds from their 529 plan. This is false. The 529 plan may be used to pay for tuition at a private college or university as well as a public state college or university. Furthermore, your child may attend any accredited degree granting educational institution.

- My child will have to attend college if I establish a 529 plan and I am not sure if he will. This is false. Even if your child decides that college is not for him you will not lose the funds in the 529 plan. We will discuss this topic later.

Here are the benefits that a 529 College Savings Plan offers:

- The account's earnings are exempt from federal tax. If you use the funds within the 529 plan to pay for your child's college expenses then no taxes are due on the proceeds from the plan. Any interest or capital gains from your original investments are entirely tax free. This is one of the 529 plan's greatest benefits.

- Many states allow you to deduct some or all of your 529 plan contributions from your state income taxes.

- There are no income limitations that might prevent you from contributing to a 529 plan for your child.

- You control the 529 plan and your child does not have access to the funds in this account. This may be an important distinction as some other ways of saving for college, such as a savings account in your child's name, could allow your child access to the money when he reaches the age of majority in your state.

- If your child decides not to go to college for some reason you may roll the 529 plan proceeds over to another family member such as a sibling, cousin, parent, etc.

- Many states do not have an age or time limit that dictates when the funds must be used.

- If your child should receive a scholarship any unused money may be withdrawn without paying the 10% penalty but you will still owe the tax on any gains.

- Anyone may contribute to a 529 plan not just the individual who opened the account. Contributions to a 529 plan also qualify for the $12,000 ($24,000 for married couples in 2006) annual gift tax exclusion.

- You may accelerate 5 years worth of contributions and put $60,000 ($120,000 for married couples in 2007) into a 529 plan.

As is always the case in life there are some drawbacks to 529 College Savings Plans:

- The 529 account is treated as an asset of the parent and may therefore affect financial aid eligibility.

- If you decide to withdraw the money from the 529 account and not use the proceeds for college expenses then you will have to pay tax as well as a 10% penalty.

- Each child must have his own 529 account. However, you are able to change the recipient in the future.

- Although you are the account owner, 529 accounts are considered gifts and are not part of your estate assets.

Many parents like the fact that they may be able to receive a state income tax deduction today by contributing to their child's 529 plan and this is a very nice benefit. However, the far greater benefit comes from the future tax treatment and not having to pay federal income taxes on the earnings when they are withdrawn to pay for qualified education expenses. This should lead you to find the best plan with the best investment options and mutual funds or Exchange Traded Funds (ETFs). While it is nice to save a few hundred dollars today by way of the state income tax deduction it will be much more beneficial for your child if he is able to receive an additional 1% or 2% per year investment return on the 529 account funds over 5, 10 or 15 years. Look for the best plan even if it is not in your state.

You will find on the internet that each year various groups and magazines publish rankings of the best and worst 529 plans throughout the country. While there are occasionally changes year to year the same states seem to come out on top each year. Remember, it is the amount you contribute (the more the better most financial planners will say) and the investment return over time that are the most important components. Do not focus solely on the state tax deduction that you will receive today.

Keep in mind that once you contribute to a 529 plan you will not be able to gain access to the money until your child attends a qualified educational institution. Should you need the money before that time you'll not only pay taxes you will also pay a 10% penalty on the amount withdrawn. Think long and hard before contributing to a 529 plan as it should be money that you do not need in the future. There is no sense putting yourself in a liquidity crunch that may cause you trouble down the road just so that you are able to contribute to your child's plan.

As always make sure that you have paid off all high interest rate credit card balances before contributing to your child's 529 plan. Also make sure that you are taking care of your own retirement before contributing to a 529 plan for your child.

UTMAs and UGMAs

The most obvious question is what is the difference between the Uniform Transfers to Minors Act (UTMA) and the Uniform Gift to Minors Act (UGMA)?

The Uniform Gift to Minors Act (UGMA) came into law first. The Uniform Transfer to Minors Act (UTMA) expands the previous law. Most states have adopted the UTMA which replaces the UGMA. Check in your state which kind of account you'll need to open. Your child will need to have a social security number in order for an account to be established. You, or another adult, will act on your child's behalf until he reaches the age of majority in your state.

Your child will own the UTMA or UGMA that you establish. At the age of majority in your state your child legally owns and controls the assets in the account.

Any unearned income that your child realizes from these accounts is subject to taxation. The IRS allows a child under 14 years of age to have $850 of unearned income (this level will probably be indexed for inflation) tax free in a calendar year.

UTMAs and UGMAs can be good investment vehicles for young people because they allow for a wide range of investment options. The funds in such accounts are usually invested in equity mutual funds but you should check with your financial advisor to see what makes the most sense. Please also look into Exchange Traded Funds (ETFs) as they can be a much cheaper alternative to mutual funds. See Appendix G for more information.

      The younger your child is the more sense it makes to invest the funds in an equity mutual fund. This is not an either or choice. There are providers that will allow for a mix of investment dollars. Some of the account's funds may be invested in mutual funds and some of the funds may be invested in fixed income assets. No matter what you decide is best for your child the aim is to obtain a greater return on investment over time than that of a savings account or a money market at a local bank. If you refer to the table on page 45 you can easily see that a few percentage points difference in the rate of return can make a big difference in the amount of money that your child will have in 10, 20 or 30 years. They also have time on their side and are able to "wait out" downturns in the equity market. This is why most financial advisors recommend that young children be substantially invested in equities through mutual funds. We'll talk more about UTMAs and UGMAs later.

How Your Child's Funds Should Be Invested

Time is your child's greatest strength when it comes to her investing plan. Whether the funds are for your child's college education, funds for her to put a down payment on a house or funds for her retirement the fact that your child has many years, if not decades ahead of her will be beneficial in two ways.

First, longer periods of time make a big difference when it comes to compounding. As we have seen the difference of as little as 5 years can make a great difference in the amount of money grows to in the future.

Second, time will allow your child to ride out the ups and downs in stock market. These ups and downs are known as volatility. Volatility is simply a measure of the swings around the average (usually yearly) return. The stock market has returned roughly 11% per year since 1930. This is less than half of the story. In some years that market was up more than 50% and in other years it was down more than 50%. That is quite a ride and this volatility scares many investors.

Some investors refuse to buy equity mutual funds because of this volatility. If an investor has two decades before he needs this invested money then he is making a poor decision in not investing in equity mutual funds because he will most likely realize a lower annual return by investing in another asset class. If the investor will need the invested money within 5 to 7 years (there is no "right" number of years) then he should be rotating out of stocks over time into fixed income.

Volatility also prompts poor short term decisions by many investors. In years where the equity mutual funds lose value many investors will sell their mutual fund holdings and move the cash into something safe such as a bank account or some other fixed income investment. Research has shown that investors sell their mutual funds at the wrong time. They usually sell when they should be buying and buy when they should be selling. During down periods in the market, if the money invested is to be held for the long term (say at least 7 years), then an investor should continue buying during this down period. This is known as "dollar cost averaging" and should improve the future outcome of the investment. By investing money on a fixed schedule, say once a month, then when a mutual fund loses value the investor will be buying shares of the mutual fund at cheaper prices

Your child's investing time horizon is listed below from the longest to the shortest:

- Retirement
- House Down Payment
- College

We will talk about ways that your child may be able to save for retirement. No matter what method you and your child decide on to save for your child's retirement it is clear that he will not be retiring for many, many decades. These retirement funds should definitely be invested for the long haul and the equity exposure should high. Although the volatility will be higher with these funds invested mainly in equity mutual funds the difference in future dollars of just an additional 1% of return per year will make a tremendous difference in the amount of retirement funds that your child has in 30, 40, 50 or 60 years!

If you have earmarked funds for your child so that he will have some money to buy a house when the time comes, this money may be invested relatively aggressively depending on your child's age. If you estimate that your child won't be buying a home for 20 or more years then most financial planners would recommend that a large portion of these funds be invested in equity mutual funds.

College savings may also be invested aggressively when your child is young. As he or she approaches college age you will need to reduce the amount of the funds that are invested in equity mutual funds. This applies to all of the above savings categories for your child. When he is ready for college you will not simply sell all of the equity mutual funds the day before he attends college and move the money into a safer investment. This would be a very, very risky strategy. Yes, you may catch an upswing in the equity market but your child's savings may be severely damaged by a year in which the equity market drops 20%, 30% or even 50%!

With all of your child's investments, whether they are for college or for a down payment on a home, you will need to ensure that money invested in equity mutual funds is slowly rotated out of the mutual funds into a safer choice. Let's take the example of Stacey, an energetic 11 year old. She will be attending college, most likely, in 6 years at the age of 17. Today, her parents have a 529 College Savings Plan for Stacey that is 100% invested in equity mutual funds. Six years seems like a long time, but not when it comes to Mr. Stock Market. Mr. Stock Market can easily be in a good or bad mood for 6 years. Stacey's parents know this and they decide on a strategy to improve the chances that Stacey's college fund grows over the next 6 years but also the risk is reduced. Her parents decide to take the following percentages out of equity mutual funds each year and shift the funds to a safer mix of short term Treasuries and CDs at their local bank.

Age   Percentage Moved out of Equity Mutual Funds

Age	Percentage
11	15%
12	15%
13	15%
14	15%
15	20%
16	20%

This is only one of many strategies and may be too aggressive for your family. Talk to your financial advisor to settle on a strategy that you are comfortable with. The goal is to slowly take money out of the equity market where it may be at risk over the time horizon of only 6 years. By the time Stacey turns 15 she has only 40% of her college funds invested in the stock market. When she turns 16, with only 1 year until she attends college, Stacey has no money in the stock market and all of the funds are in safe investments.

Stacey may not need 100% of her college funds the day she starts college. She may have another 3 or 4 years before she will need some of the funds and this provides additional time to rotate the money out of the equity mutual funds into safe investments.

What to Expect

Your child should be invested in the stock market in a mutual fund or funds that provide broad exposure for funds that he will not need for at least several years as was discussed previously. The game of investing in the stock market over long periods of time comes down to:

- Average annual return and the return seen over shorter periods of time
- The intra-period drawdown (we'll talk more about this concept which is an easy one to understand but sounds complicated!)
- Investing on a regular basis
- Doing nothing

Depending on what period of history you look at the stock market has returned on average 11% over the last 50 years. This is an approximate number and the figure is different depending on the time period you look at and the stock market sector you are tracking. Small cap stocks, large cap stocks and international stocks have different historical returns. While we are not being specific and simply talking about the stock market as a whole please, please search out the best investment in your opinion so that you child's money has the greatest chance to grow. Do not settle for 1% or 2% less. Once again, let's look at the difference between receiving an 8%, 10%, 12% and 14% average annual return over 15 years on $2,000 invested today:

	In 15 Years	**% Difference**
8%	$6,344	-
10%	$8,353	+32%
12%	$10,947	+31%
14%	$14,276	+30%

These are tremendous differences. If your child is able to achieve an annual average return of 10% instead of 8% over 15 years he will have $8,353 in 15 years which is 32% more than the $6,344 realized at 8%. The differences, in dollar terms, are even greater when the amount of money invested increases and/or the time over which the money is invested is greater.

Let's take a look at the recent annual returns of the Standard & Poors (S&P) 500 since this bench mark is used by many financial professional:

Year	**Return**
2007	+5.36% (through December 26th)
2006	+12.80%
2005	+3.01%
2004	+9.00%
2003	+26.39%
2002	-23.37%
2001	-13.04%
2000	-10.14%
1999	+19.51%
1998	+26.67%
1997	+31.02%
1996	+20.27%

This simple chart shows us several things. The first is that $100 invested at the beginning of 1996 would have grown to $228.66 over this period of time. This chart shows that the return by year varies tremendously. In 1997 the return for the year was +31.02% which put many people in a very good mood. The return in 2002 was -23.37% and this probably put many people in a very bad mood. This poor return in 2002 followed two previous years of losses as well! Imagine if one had been invested 100% in stocks at the beginning of 2000 and needed the money at the end of 2002. If they had started with $10,000 they would have only had $5,988!

This is why stock market investing works best if you have time on your side. The greater the period of time the funds are invested the more likely it is that the money will grow rather than shrink. You can see that the "intra-period drawdown" or the amount that an investment can decrease in a period (in this case a year) can be very significant. The chart below is very interesting because it focuses on the worst case scenario over a period of time:

%Stocks	Worst Month	Worst 12 Months	Worst 36 Months	Worst 50 Months
0	-4.8%	-4.8%	0.9%	17.4%
10	-4.5%	-4.0%	8.2%	26.0%
20	-5.1%	-5.7%	6.3%	27.4%
30	-5.7%	-9.8%	2.6%	26.0%
40	-6.4%	-13.7%	-1.1%	21.2%
50	-7.2%	-17.5%	-4.7%	16.5%
60	-9.3%	-21.2%	-8.2%	11.7%
70	-11.4%	-24.8%	-11.7%	7.0%
80	-13.5%	-28.2%	-15.1%	2.3%
90	-15.6%	-31.6%	-18.4%	-2.3%
100	-17.7%	-34.8%	-21.7%	-6.9%

The first column is the percentage of an investment account that is invested in the stock market. The remaining three columns show the worst 12, 36 and 50 month periods. This chart is based on historical data going back to 1920. For example, if an account was 100% invested in stocks and experienced the worst 12 months in the stock market that has been seen to date then the account would lose 34.8% of its value during that time. Over the worst 36 months, or 3 years, that account would have lost 21.7% of its value and over 50 months it would have lost 6.9% of its value. This chart should help you to understand that the way to really get hurt when investing in the stock market is to do the following:

Not allowing enough time to invest. We have seen time and time again that the best, and easiest, way to invest in the stock market is to invest early, keep investing and hold your investments for long periods of time. Trying to make money quickly in the stock market is a very, very hard game to win and far more people have lost than have won.

Not slowly shifting money out of the stock market into safer investments long before you will need the money. As we see in the chart above, even 50 months, if your account is 100% invested in stocks may not be enough time to recover from a poor stock market. After waiting 50 months (4 years and 2 months) your account would still be down 6.9%! Make sure that you start shifting money out long before you will need it. If you had put the money in a safe investment at a 5% yearly return you'd be up over 20% before taxes!

Invest on a Regular Basis

Untold sums of money and energy have been spent over the last 100 years trying to figure out the stock market and find some way to beat it. Several things have been learned from these endeavors. Yes, an incredibly small number of people seem to be able to predict where the stock market is going over short periods of time. These people are not always the same year after year. In one year a particular person may correctly predict the direction of the stock market and then he won't correctly predict the direction of the market for another 5 years or a lifetime. And these are people whose full time job it is to figure out where the stock market is going! They spend an enormous amount of time and effort to try to predict its direction.

Most of us do not have the time or energy to do what most of the professionals cannot just as most of us have neither the time, ability or wherewithal to play professional sports better than the pros. Most of us will need to invest in the stock market not knowing what it will do in the future. That is OK because there are several things you can do to improve your chances of earning money while investing your funds in the stock market.

The first is to invest on a regular basis. Whether it is in a 401(k) plan, a 529 Plan or simply a mutual fund account in your name investing a little bit each month or even twice a year will help to reduce the fluctuations over time in your account. When you invest a fixed dollar amount every month, say $100, when the market is high and your chosen mutual fund is more expensive you will be buying fewer shares of that mutual. The reverse is true when the market is down and you are able to buy more shares of the mutual fund with the $100 investment.

The Importance of Doing Nothing

Usually, doing nothing is a sure recipe for disaster when it comes to most things in our lives. Investing in the stock market actually requires this of investors IF they have time on their side to invest. Doing nothing can be hard for most of us. Humans seem to be built to take action especially when something bad is happening such as a declining stock market that is slowly eating away at the value of our investments. During such periods you must stick with your plan for investing and know that you have time on your side. You should keep contributing to your investment accounts and benefit from dollar cost averaging by buying shares in mutual funds more cheaply than you were able to when the market was at higher levels. Some of history's greatest investors have said that their ability to sit and wait was the most important element of their investing success.

One of the worst things investors do is to become scared and then sell out of their mutual funds at the bottom of a stock market cycle only to miss the upside as the market recovers. To invest in the stock market you have to come to terms with the fact that your investment, and those you make for your child, will fluctuate. The investments will be up in some years and down in other years. History tells us that over time the funds grow even if they do so in an erratic way. Don't get scared out of the market on the way down. Opportunity is often best when things seem the worst.

You may have experienced the wild ride in the stock market or maybe you have not. You will need to work hard to do nothing when the market drops. It seems to go against our nature. If you can master this skill you will find the other aspects of investing in the stock market to be relatively easy.

Pillar Four: Multiple Streams of Income

Whether you feel that uncertainty is undesirable or that the greater opportunity it sparks is beneficial, one thing is for certain, jobs today are not as secure as they were during the previous generation. Your child will grow up in a world where very, very few people will stay with the same company for 25 years. In fact, many people will change jobs every three to seven years depending on their age. Young people may change jobs as frequently as every two to three years. Many of these job changes are positive events for the employee because he found a better, higher paying job that will be more satisfying. However, some of these job changes will be due to downsizing and layoffs. The older workers, those 45 years and older, are most at risk because they are the most expensive and sometimes viewed as less adaptable and less hard working than the younger workers. Ironically, it is these older workers who usually need an income the most as their financial obligations are often the greatest.

There are many statistics on the future of the workforce and job opportunities. Many experts envision that those who are twenty one years of age and are entering the workforce will not only have six to ten different jobs during thirty plus years of working, they are very likely to have three to five distinctly different careers. What exactly does this mean? It means that someone who starts out as an engineer helping to design computer chips could easily wind up also running a business and becoming a financial journalist before he retires. This potential path is far different from that of previous generations. This opportunity and uncertainty is driven by three different factors and it is important that your child understand each of them:

- Complexity
- Change
- Speed

Many of the jobs that younger people will hold in ten years do not even exist today. In fact, many of the jobs that are prevalent today did not exist a decade ago. There are more different kinds of jobs today than ever before. DVD players, cell phones, computers, health care products and many other products and industries have created tens of thousands of jobs that did not exist even a short time ago. This is a sign of complexity. Our economy is more complex that it has ever been and that complexity will increase. It provides wonderful opportunities for workers who have the proper education and background to take advantage of these opportunities. Complexity requires that your child is well educated and adaptable. These are traits that are necessary for him to acquire and keep a good paying job. He will need to update his skills throughout his career to stay competitive. This complexity in the economy will also offer more opportunities than ever for your child to achieve multiple sources of income.

Encourage your child to embrace complexity in today's world as it offers tremendous opportunity for him or her to become knowledgeable in an area and then use this knowledge to create a career that is enjoyable and profitable. You children should not be afraid of complexity. The best way for them to handle complexity is to build a secure financial base so that they are able to capitalize on the opportunities that complexity presents in the future.

Change has always been a part of life and it is a very large part of economies and entire industries. New industries and businesses rise up to take advantage of new opportunities while older businesses and industries decline and eventually disappear. This phenomenon is driven by new technologies that displace old technologies. The car eventually replaced the horse and the buggy. More recently, electronic trading completely displaced the typical trading floor of one of Europe's largest exchanges in just about one year. Cell phones are slowly replacing the typical home telephone and saving for retirement has now become the employee's responsibility rather than the employer's.

Our children today seem more attuned to change and more comfortable with it. It is important that they understand that change is part of life and is not necessarily a bad thing. The results of this change can certainly be bad or good, but the important point for your children is that the more prepared they are and the better their education and training the better they will be able to navigate the sea of change and take advantage of its many opportunities.

The speed at which the economy moves is not only great, but the rate at which this speed is increasing appears to be increasing as well. Many older people intuitively sense that things move much more quickly today than they did in the past. In fact, there appears to be a social requirement that things move quickly. Companies strive to provide products and services to the customer as quickly as possible. There is emphasis on how quickly things can get done. The speed at which new ideas and new products enter the marketplace is truly amazing. It used to take some products five years to make it to market. Today, similar products are often brought to market in less than six months.

The combination of complexity, change and speed offer tremendous opportunity for highly skilled workers. It also provides a heavy burden, at times, on these workers. The 9 to 5 workday seems to have faded into the background over the last twenty years. The demands of complexity, change and speed require that workers rise to the challenge of these forces. This can lead to long hours, stress and friction at home.

Hopefully, your child will find a career and employment that he or she enjoys and provides financial comfort. It is more likely today than ever before that your child will succeed financially and have a good job if she properly prepares herself. If "dying of boredom" was one of the greatest worries of white collar workers in the 60s, 70s and the early 80s, the greatest concern now is being "worked to death." How should your child insure against the world of complexity, change and speed? The same way that wealthy people have for generations. Your child should strive to realize multiple streams of income.

The prevailing wisdom of parents for the last few generations may be summed up as follows:

- Study hard in school so that you get into a good college
- Study hard in college so that you get a good job
- Work hard in your job so that you get promoted and repeat this process

This is certainly good advice. One difference between the middle, upper middle class and the wealthy is that wealthy people tend to diversify income as well as assets.

We hear much on the topic of diversifying our assets and that we should not put all of our eggs into one basket. A sound investment portfolio should contain stocks, bonds, real estate and other assets to diversify. This should improve returns and reduce risk. Very little is mentioned on the topic of diversifying income. However, diversification of income is as important if not more important than diversifying assets. This is something that separates the wealthy form the middle class. The wealthy derive income from many, often times unrelated sources. When one source of income decreases or disappears the others should compensate. Many times a particular stream of income becomes a real winner and provides healthy returns for years to come.

When your child is working full time it will be very difficult for him to create multiple streams of income by working multiple jobs. This should not be the aim. There are only twenty fours in a day and seven days in a week. The foundation for multiple streams of income for young people is to start with solid employment. This is an active source of income that requires showing up everyday and putting in a certain number of hours. The other sources of income will require some time but should strive to obtain leverage to produce returns. A few examples of good, passive, income producing activities are:

- Residential rental properties
- Commercial properties
- Web based and small businesses
- A passive investment in someone else's businesses
- Fixed income investments

Residential Rental Properties

A prime method of creating a passive income stream is to own rental property. A lot of work will go into identifying, researching and purchasing a property. Once the property is purchased it will, if the tenants are carefully chosen, require little time and certainly won't require time on a daily basis. Occasionally, the property will require effort on your child's part. This effort may be needed to repair some part of the rental property or find someone who will perform the repair. Time and effort may be required on occasion to find tenants to replace those who are leaving. However, on a daily basis the property will create cash flow and will appreciate as real estate prices increase. This is the real power of using rental properties to create another stream of income.

Let's take a look at a simple example. If Dave, a 25 year old, is gainfully employed and has been saving diligently he will have money to invest. One day, while driving home from work, Dave stumbles upon a for sale sign in a condominium complex. The next day he calls the listing realtor and then goes to see the property. The unit is a 2 bedroom condo that is in good condition in an appealing part of town. The seller is asking for $220,000. Dave does some research and learns that he would be able to rent this condominium for $1,800 a month. He determines that he can afford to put 20% as a down payment on the property.

Dave contacts the listing agent and offers $190,000 for the property. Dave knows that the best way to buy any property is to not be anxious and approach investment properties as a business. This knowledge gives Dave the confidence to bid well below the asking price. The seller comes back and counters with an asking price of $200,000. Dave has done his homework and run the figures so he is comfortable paying $200,000 for the condo. The sale closes about 2 months later and at that time Dave has two tenants for the property. They each will pay $900 a month. Here is what Dave has calculated:

$200,000 Purchase Price
$40,000 Down payment
$160,000 Mortgage at 6.00%

Here are the ongoing monthly expenses:

$960 Mortgage
$200 Homeowners Association Fee
$200 Property Tax

The total for all of these expenses is $1,360. The total rent is $1,800 a month which reflects two tenants each paying $900 a month. On a pure cashflow basis, Dave will have $440 of income each month.

There will be months where maintenance will be required and Dave will see less than $440, but he is comfortable with this. One great advantage of buying condominiums rather than single family homes as investment properties is that as a condominium owner, Dave is only responsible for the maintenance on the inside of the unit. The Homeowners Association will take care of all of the outside maintenance such as cutting the lawn, trimming the trees and painting the exterior of the building. The Homeowners Association also will normally be responsible for replacing an old roof and maintaining the gutters and the exterior of the structure.

Dave also profits from a benefit that the IRS grants to landlords known as depreciation. The IRS stipulates that an owner who rents his property must depreciate the building (not the land) over 27.5 years. Dave has an appraisal done on the condominium and the appraiser determines that 65% of the $200,000 value comes from the value of the building. The remaining 35% of the purchase price is the value of the land. Dave is able to depreciate $130,000, 65% of $200,000, over 27.5 or $4,727 per year. This depreciation amount of $4,727 is deducted from the income that Dave receives in a year.

At $440 a month, Dave has an income of $5,280 a year from this rental property. He is now allowed to deduct the depreciation amount of $4,727 from the $5,280 worth of income leaving him with only $553 of taxable income from his investment property.

The $4,727 of depreciation is not a cash expense that reduces the money that Dave actually receives from the property. It is simply a "phantom expense" that reduces Dave's income tax. If Dave is in the 25% income tax bracket then he pays 25% of $553 or $138.25. This means that Dave's after tax income from the property is $5,280 - $138.25 or $5,141.75.

Dave originally invested $40,000 in the property as his down payment. Dave's after tax return on investment is $5,141.75 divided by $40,000 or 12.85%. This is very attractive. But, the picture is even better when the appreciation on the property is taken into account.

Real estate prices nationally have increased around 5% over the last three decades. In any one year, this price appreciation could be higher or lower than the average. If Dave expects to keep his investment property for many years, his average annual return should be about 5%. 5% of $200,000 is $10,000 in Dave's first year of ownership. Not only did Dave realize the $5,141.75 of after tax income from the rental property he also saw $10,000 of price appreciation for a total of $15,141.75 or a return of +37.8% on his original investment.

If real estate prices increase by 5% a year for the next 20 years, Dave's condo will be worth around $530,659 when Dave is 45 and $1,407,997 when Dave turns 65 years old. This is a tremendous boost to Dave's net worth and all for an original investment of $40,000. This does not even take into account the after tax, passive income stream that Dave realizes for 40 years and the increases in rent that occur during that period of time.

It is easy to see why real estate is still the number one producer of wealth and most wealthy people are able to point to real estate in some form that has made them wealthy. The leverage inherent in real estate, assuming some money is borrowed, enhances returns. Dave clearly was not able to pay $200,000 in cash for the rental property because he did not have this much money in savings. Dave only had a little more than $40,000 to invest. By taking out a mortgage and borrowing $160,000 from the bank Dave was able to own a $200,000 property. The 5% price appreciation Dave realized during the first year was on $200,000 or $10,000. $8,000 of this $10,000 appreciation came from the $160,000 that Dave borrowed from the bank. This phenomenon of leverage is also known as using "Other People's Money."

The best time for your child to take advantage of real estate is when it is out of favor with the general public. The last few years have seen tremendous interest in real estate amongst the public and investment properties that make sense and are good investments are few and far between. That will change eventually. There are always investment opportunities but they change from time to time. Always the best time to invest is when that asset class is out of favor and undervalued.

If you and your child decide that rental properties are right up your alley, please do as much research as possible and make sure that your child learns all he can about the process of selecting and buying investment properties. A good real estate broker that knows the local area will go a long way in helping your child uncover properties that make sense for investment. Several things must come together to make an investment property a good investment for your child.

First, the property must fit your child's personality and he or she must be comfortable running and/or overseeing the property. For example, if your daughter is a straight laced, laid back person she may not want to own an investment in a tough part of town with a lot of rough characters for tenants no matter how good an investment it appears to be.

Second, tenants will make or break an investment property. While the property and its characteristics are very important, at the end of the day the tenants are the most important part of a rental property. Unfortunately, the quality of your future tenants cannot be calculated when you run the numbers on an investment property. If you have good tenants that stay for a long period of time, pay their rent on time and keep the property in good shape, your child will spend almost no effort during any given year in tending to the investment. Young families with children tend to stay in rental properties for only short periods of time as they usually want to buy a home of their own. Tenants with children also are harder on a property and there are usually greater costs associated with more frequent painting and tending to small repairs.

Some of the best tenants are older. They tend to stay in a property for fairly long stretches and generally do not wreck the property. When your child is researching investment properties a very important factor in the decision making process is determining what kind of tenants a particular property will attract. Will it attract young families or very young people who spend a lot of time partying?

Finding the right property that is a good fit for your child will require that he spend time looking for listings and visiting some properties. This is part of being financially aware and looking for opportunities in all aspects of life. It is a level of awareness that will keep your child looking for opportunities at all times. This constant effort, even if it yields only one or two quality properties over a 10 year period, will have a dramatic effect on your child's future well being.

There are many excellent books that cover investing in residential investment properties. Please learn as much as possible before venturing into any sizeable investment.

Commercial Properties

Commercial properties are those where the tenants are businesses instead of individuals. The area of commercial properties presents its own challenges and opportunities and usually investors in this area gained experience by investing in residential properties first.

Commercial properties also behave differently than residential properties and can be a good way to diversify. Often times when the residential property market is weak the commercial market is hot and vice versa. Commercial property investments, and residential property investments, help to diversify a portfolio because real estate is an asset class. When other asset classes, such as stocks and bonds, are down real estate may be going up.

There are many subtle details when it comes to investing in real estate and commercial properties in particular. There are many good books that delve into these details and if you are interested you should do further research. But, we will point out a few important items.

When a bank loans money for the purchase of a commercial property it is much more interested in the property than it is in the buyer. This is very different from the purchase of real estate that the buyer plans to occupy. In this case, the bank is very interested in the buyer's income, the buyer's credit rating and the buyer's ability to pay back the mortgage in a timely fashion. The banks also are very interested in the buyer when an investment property is being purchased.

Banks view commercial properties in a slightly different light. While your bank will want to ensure that you have the ability to properly manage a commercial property and pay back the mortgage the bank gives you something of a break. The bank will look very closely to determine if the commercial property creates enough cashflow to cover the mortgage and all other ongoing expenses. If this is the case then the buyer has some wiggle room with respect to his income and credit rating.

Commercial properties also offer many of the same tax benefits, and some others, that residential properties offer. These tax considerations are very powerful and really help build wealth over the long term. As always, discuss the tax consequences of any investment with your financial advisor.

Tax Free Money and the 1031 Exchange

Real Estate has been a tremendous wealth creator. Today, it has the traditional appeal that, over time, real estate tends to appreciate and by using leverage intelligently your child will be able to magnify these returns on his investment. There are also advantages to owning income producing properties. Practically all expenses incurred in running the property are deductible against income for tax purposes. Depreciation also makes it more likely that a particular income property will produce positive cashflow. These are only some of the fantastic benefits of owning income producing properties. As if this was not enough there are two very powerful tools that your child may employ in intelligently using real estate to his advantage.

One may create tax free funds by allowing one to refinance a property and take cash out while doing so. Let's take an example of a $200,000 rental property with an existing $150,000 mortgage. This property produces $700 a month after all expenses are paid, hence it is said to be "cash flow positive" to the tune of $700 a month. If your child sees another terrific investment he may go the bank that holds the current $150,000 mortgage and ask for a $200,000 mortgage. Your child has done the calculation and figures that the additional mortgage will cost him $300 a month. This means that his positive cash flow will drop to $400 from $700 a month because he will have a $200,000 mortgage on the rental property instead of a $150,000 mortgage. Your child decides that this is worth it as he has identified a great investment property that he will need to put a down payment of $50,000 on. Your child will pay no tax on the $50,000 check he receives from the bank! If he had sold the property instead taxes would be due but by taking advantage of the cash out refinance (refi) he will pay no taxes. What a fantastic way to build wealth. The critical thing that your child needs to keep in mind when taking advantage of a cash out refi is that the money must be used to invest and buy an appreciating asset. Cash out refis have become very popular as interest rates have been dropping and the value of most real estate has been climbing. Unfortunately, most people who take money out of their homes in this way make the huge mistake of buying assets that depreciate such as TVs, cars and boats. This is a big mistake. Their monthly mortgage payment goes up and they destroy this wealth by buying things that go down in value over time.

Even if your child decided to sell his rental property he may not have to pay any taxes! If he identifies a better (more expensive) property then he may roll the proceeds of the sale into this larger property and pay no taxes at all! This is known as a 1031 Exchange. No wonder real estate has produced more millionaires to date than any other investment vehicle. There are many rules and restrictions with respect to a 1031 Exchange so make sure to seek the help of a competent professional.

Web Based and Small Businesses

The internet has changed the way we live and work. That is no surprise. Most people also realize that any technology or process that substantially changes our lives for the better usually provides fantastic investing opportunities. What most people don't realize is how many small businesses were created with the internet as their sole source of advertising and distribution.

I know someone who loved fly fishing and enjoyed tying flies for his fishing trips. He was able to start a business online and now sells his hand tied flies all over the world. He has had some customers for over 7 years. There was a story written about an individual who has been collecting refrigerator magnets since he was a child. This hobby has grown into a full time business.

One of my first web ventures was based on a true niche market. Our firm sold bat detectors. What is a bat detector? A bat detector is a small, handheld device that allows the user to hear the sounds that bats make as they hunt the night sky for insects. Bats use echolocation which is a fancy name for radar to locate flying bugs and navigate. These sounds cannot be heard by the human ear as the frequencies are too high. You may learn more by visiting www.econvergence.net/batdet.htm If bat detectors can be sold on the internet I am willing to bet that almost anything can be sold as well.

There are many benefits to small, web based businesses. Here are just a few:

- Take a hobby or some interest that you have and translate it into a revenue generating endeavor.
- Low startup costs. Where else can you setup shop and advertise your products for a small sum of money. Web hosting companies have very low fees for hosting your website and credit card merchant services are truly inexpensive as well.
- Advertising can be as cheap or as expensive as you want it to. Yes, you can pay for banner ads and spend large sums of money to do so and in some cases this is the way to go. However, you can also write articles, get linked to sites that are related to your product, start a blog or get mentioned in an online e-zine. Many of these methods will require no out of pocket expense.
- Whether your child is a techie or not no longer matters. The web hosting companies have made it so easy to build a website that your child does not have to be a programmer to establish a web business. There are also many individuals that charge a few hundred dollars to build a website.
- Another source of income.
- The pride of building a business from the ground up and being a business owner.
- Significant tax breaks and benefits that are not available to employees. We will talk about this topic many times throughout this book. From a tax perspective it is far better to be a business owner than an employee.

Your child's first step is to find a product or service that the business will be centered around. The second step is marketing and getting the word out. I cannot stress enough the importance of this step. Whether it is working to improve search engine rankings or working on paid advertising campaigns your child will need to make sure that potential customers are aware of the product. Remember, a business is not a business until it has sales. I have seen too many entrepreneurs focus on the wrong things. They spend a lot of time worrying about setting up an LLC or a corporation, selecting a name for their business, getting business cards and stationary and setting up a business checking account. Most of these tasks are entirely unimportant.

Your child should worry only about creating sales and driving revenue. Everything else is secondary and unnecessary if there are no sales. Your child should only worry about any subsequent steps until sales are being made. Once a website is up and running all energy should be focused on creating sales. During this period your child should pay for expenses personally. Many experienced entrepreneurs at this stage don't even have a business checking account or a business credit card.

The most important task at this point in the business is to determine if the business is viable and will make money. As little money as possible should be spent on things other than marketing and advertising at this point. Once the business shows that it can turn a profit then the other issues may be addressed so that your child is able to realize the income from the venture.

Many successful entrepreneurs strive to keep all costs that are not related to marketing as low as possible. They spend money only when they absolutely have to. They have not incorporated or established a structure for their business. You may be asking how it is possible to run a business if all parts of the business are not in place.

These successful entrepreneurs often do not have a bank account or a structure established for their business. They often times will take orders, collect a credit card number or a check payable to a business that does not yet exist. Your child may speak to customers on the phone and take their shipping address and credit card information. Your child should either then ship the product or inform the customer in a few days that the product is no longer available and that their credit card will not be charged. Checks may be made out to a business name even if that name does not exist. Again, your child may decide to pay out of pocket to ship the order to create goodwill or may return the check to the customer and inform him that the product is no longer available. Once the business shows that it is able to turn a profit, even if it is just a few hundred dollars a month, then your child should go about establishing a bank account, a merchant account and a business credit card.

The first step is to setup a business entity. Appendix C lists many resources to help in this endeavor. There are companies that will setup a business entity for a small fee. You and your child should discuss with a competent advisor the structure that is best suited to your child's web business. Many entrepreneurs decide to establish an S corporation, as opposed to a C corporation, because of the ease of establishing an S corporation, the liability protection and the reduced chance of an audit. Other business entities include a sole proprietorship, C corporation, Limited Liability Company (LLC) and Limited Partnership (LLP). There are pros and cons to each entity and this is why the options must be discussed with your financial advisor or attorney.

In many ways obtaining a bank account is difficult. The business entity must be established first and have an Employer Identification Number (EIN) or, for sole proprietorships, your child's Social Security Number must be used. Your child should go to the bank where he or she already has a personal banking relationship. This will help in establishing accounts for the business. Your child's business will need a savings account and a checking account. A business incurs many expenses. Some of them are anticipated and some are not. Your child will need the flexibility to meet these expenses in the best way possible. This is why a credit card will also be needed.

Once the business has established accounts at a bank and the business entity is established it is relatively easy for your child to obtain a credit card for the company. In many cases the credit card company will insist on having your child's credit back the credit card. If your child is the only one with spending authority on the account then this is no problem. After a period of time your child should seek to have this link lifted. The more separation between personal and business financial matters the better in all cases.

Investing in Other Businesses

Just as your child may start his or her own business your child may also be offered the opportunity to invest in a business started by one of their peers. The investment may require either a passive or an active role in the company. Your child should seek whatever role he or she feels is the best fit.

This area of investing can be risky but the payoffs may be large as well. The aim in this type of investing is to create an income stream into the future. Your child should make sure that his goals match those of the founders and those who run the company. Some companies have the goal of becoming economically viable ongoing concerns while others have the stated intent to grow to a point where they will be sold and all of the investors and owners paid out at the time.

The Best Tax Break Around: Owning a Business

Most people do not realize a simple fact. There are two tax systems in the United States. The first system is for employees. The second system is for employers also known as business owners. Now, which do you think is better? The tax system that applies to business owners is far more favorable than that applied to employees. The primary reason is that business owners are able to pay themselves first.

As an employee, I would pay taxes in the following manner:

Earnings – Taxes Due = Paycheck

The government collects taxes before I receive any money. I never even see the money that the government collects as it is withheld from my paycheck. Now, the tax system for a business owner is very different:

Earnings – Expenses = Profit (taxes are paid on this Profit)

This is a very subtle difference but essentially the business owner pays all expenses, including salaries and contributions to retirement plans, before the government collects any taxes! A business owner should always follow the rules when expensing items but a competent tax professional ensures that the business owner has access to all of the legally allowed deductions and qualified expenses to reduce profit so that taxes paid are minimized. An employee has no such flexibility. Furthermore, the retirement plans that a business owner has access to allow for far greater contributions than those an employee can access.

Starting and/or owning a business is very hard work. Many businesses fail and some seem to go on forever without really providing any substantial income. However, the flip side of owning a business is there are many, many tax benefits that allow the business owner's wealth to grow more rapidly than that of an employee with the same level of earnings.

Other Thoughts on Multiple Streams of Income

The risk of any an investment must be considered at all times. Any investing program should begin with a foundation of safe investments and then additional investments that take on more and more risk seeking greater returns. At all times your child should know the difference between money he needs to live, savings that are to be held in safe investment vehicles and risk capital.

Risk capital is a subset of savings and is money that is definitely not needed to live and not needed as safe savings. Risk capital is to be deployed to achieve a high return. Any investment in risk capital should be money that your child can afford to lose because some investments do become worthless or lose significant value. While most people focus on the return of a potential venture the more prudent path is to thoroughly understand the risks associated with any investment, manage them well and then often times the return takes care of itself.

One of the benefits that multiple streams of income provide is that of diversification. If your child has three sources of income, she is in better shape to weather a financial downturn. If she loses her job, and primary income stream, for six months her two investment properties will help her pay the bills during this period of time. When searching for income streams make sure that your child keeps in mind how related the streams are.

If your child works as an engineer helping to design chips for computers she should look for income streams that are not related to her primary job and her industry. If she owns an investment property in the area where she works and that area's main employment is designing chips for computers then she may be vulnerable. If her industry takes a multi-year downturn, she may lose her job and the value of her investment property may decrease at the same time. The solution may not be to sell the investment property but to create other streams of income that are not related to the technology interest.

If your daughter has always enjoyed making unique decorations for the home she may want to consider applying her talent to producing, or have someone else produce, these decorations and then sell them online via a website. She may start a dog walking businesses amongst clients that are employed in different industries. She may decide to get the business up and running and then have a full time manager run the business and your daughter can simply keep tabs on the ongoing operation. The aim is to build income streams that are not related to each other. This also allows your daughter to take advantage of trends in business. One of her income streams may all of the sudden take off because real estate becomes hot or it becomes fashionable to have someone walk your dog.

Creating multiple streams of income is mostly a mindset. Most people land a job and begin a career and use most of their mental energy to improve their position in their career of choice. This, of course, must be done. But, your child should strive to always be on the lookout for good investment opportunities and chances to create another source of income. The more passive this source is the better if your child wants to focus most of his time and energy on his chosen career. Looking for such opportunities will require time and effort that many young people use for relaxing, watching TV and going to the movies. These are all important activities that should be part of life. True freedom will come from obtaining multiple sources of income that will give your child the option to do almost anything he or she wants.

The ultimate goal in creating multiple streams of income is to have your child achieve a level of passive income that fully pays all of his or her living expenses. Living expenses are to be defined as every penny that your child spends to live including housing costs, the cost of food, transportation costs, etc. These are the costs that your child incurs before doing anything else in life.

Pillar Five: Wealth Building

It has been a long journey to this point and many people never make it to Pillar Five in their own financial lives but this is where your child is able to truly increase his net worth and build wealth. With a solid foundation of earning, saving, investing and growing those investments and creating multiple streams of income your child is now ready to take advantage of his position and build his wealth.

Most children over the past several decades were taught that they needed to work hard in school so that they could obtain good jobs. Many parents, breathing a sigh of relief, were proud when their child finally completed his schooling and landed his first full time job. As a parent you know that it takes a tremendous amount of effort to get a child to this point. Historically, most parents felt that at this point their work was done. Junior was finished with school, working at his first job and possibly out of the house. Most parents feel an admixture of pride, freedom and longing as they see their child pass into the next stage of life. It couldn't possibly be this easy, could it? A lot depends on how you view the situation.

Having your child work hard in school, identify what he likes and then chart a course to find a career doing something he loves is critically important and is good advice for any young person. There is nothing wrong with stopping at this point. Your child has a good chance of living a good, wholesome life if he manages his money wisely and keeps spending relative to income under control. You and your child should also know that there is also another universe. You and your child may choose to step into this new universe or to stay where you are. There is no right or wrong answer as this is one of these "life choices." The "right" answer differs for each family and each family must decide how to proceed.

What we do know is that there are great differences in the way wealthy people and middle class people conduct their financial lives. We have already seen that most wealthy people derive income from varied, and usually uncorrelated, multiple streams of income. This not only ensures a greater total level of income it also lessens the chance that the loss of one source of income will be devastating. Most middle class people have one source, or an overwhelmingly large source, of income. This source of income is usually wage income. In some families both parents work. In some families only one parent works and in some families there is only one parent to work. Families in which there is only parent working and this is the only or the major source of the families' income are especially vulnerable to fluctuations in the economy.

Another major difference between the wealthy and those who are less wealthy is that the wealthy, while concerned about income, are primarily concerned about their wealth which is essentially their net worth. Income and wealth are two very different things. Many people either confuse these two terms or decide not to make a distinction. Is someone who earns $1 million a year wealthy? Many people would say that this person is most certainly rich. It is impossible to tell because we don't have enough information to properly answer the question.

What if I told you that this person, while earning $1 million a year, has a net worth that is negative $20 million. This person is not rich. This person has a negative net worth that is 20 times his pre-tax annual income! It may take him 30 or 40 years to have a zero, rather than negative, net worth if he depends only on his income. This example illustrates the difference between income and wealth (net worth). Always remember that while they are often related (it is easier to have a higher net worth with a higher income) net worth and income are two distinctly different aspects of your child's financial life.

If you and your child decide that following in the footsteps of those who came before you and became wealthy there are many things that you are able to do to build wealth. The keys to building and increasing your child's wealth are as follows:

- Earning (Income)
- Increasing income and creating multiple streams of income
- Pay yourself first
- Saving and increasing the level of savings over time
- Creating a safe haven for a portion of savings
- Allocating some savings for Risk Capital
- Using Scale
- Using Leverage

By now, the first four points should look very, very familiar. It goes without saying that in order to build wealth your child will need an income and will need to save at least a portion of that income. He should also strive to increase his income and create multiple sources of income. As his total income grows he should also increase the rate at which he saves. If he starts earning $20,000 and saves 10% of his income when his income reaches $60,000 he should strive to save more than 10% of this income each year. It may seem like it would be easy to save more than 10% of income at $60,000 a year to someone earning $25,000 today. It is not nearly this easy.

Usually, as our incomes increase our expenses increase at least as fast. If they increase faster, for extended periods of time, then there is a real problem and a total overhaul of one's finances are in order. The more common problem is that as someone's income increases their expenses increase at the same rate. The result is that the percentage of income saved stays the same or drops. Without your child tracking expenses and keeping tabs on his net worth statement he may not notice the change and is very likely to be unable to explain why there was a change and what caused it.

Your child must always remember to pay himself first. If your child receives a promotion and a 10% raise then he should immediately make sure that his automatic savings plan is adjusted by the amount of the raise. If your child was saving 15% of his income and then receives a 10% raise he should increase his savings rate to

16.5% (15% + 10% of 15% = 16.5%). It cannot be stated strongly enough that if there is one rule that you and your child should follow for building wealth it is this one. Your child should always save a portion of his earnings. As his earnings increase he should increase his level of savings more than his level of expenses. This is the foundation that must be in place for building wealth over the long term. Exercising this discipline will not only build your child's wealth it will also teach him that sacrifices must be made in life to make progress and that, generally, there are no shortcuts to reaching one's financial goal.

As your child begins to save money he will need to place these savings somewhere. We have already discussed the powerful options available today for automatic savings. Your child should have money immediately and automatically placed in a savings account as soon as he receives his paycheck. If David receives $800 on the 15th and 30th of each month, he may signup with one of the online banks (see Appendix D) and have $100 withdrawn from his checking account on the following day so that he is saving $200 each month. This is a fantastic way to save money and is usually very easy as many employers now pay employees via Direct Deposit where a paycheck is directly deposited into a checking account electronically.

How should this money be invested? If saving a certain portion of your child's income is the first step to building wealth then creating a safety net for the uncertainty of life and having several months of living expenses in a safe investment is the second step. The online banks in Appendix D are perfect candidates. The money is already in your child's online bank's account. If your child has selected a Savings Account or a Money Market Account then he will receive a decent, safe return. These accounts are FDIC insured up to $100,000 and are a perfect place for his "safe money." Most financial experts recommend that a young adult have 3 to 6 months worth of living expenses in a safe account that will not fluctuate in value. This will allow your child to deal with unexpected future events such as unexpected expenses or the short term loss of a job or income.

Once your child has this solid foundation of saving a portion of his income and a safe account with 3 to 6 months worth of living expenses he or she will need to focus on building his wealth. As long as your child is consistently saving money he will build wealth over time. His savings may only be invested at 5% in a safe account but he will build wealth in the decades to come. Most financial experts recommend that young people have a safe account with 3 to 6 months worth of living expenses. Financial planners also recommend that young people take a little more risk with any additional savings they have. The level of risk will depend on your child and his risk tolerance. There are many ways for the average person to use his risk capital to grow wealth. Once of the best and easiest to learn is buying stocks in fast growing companies.

When a new trend or fad hits most people see an opportunity to spend money and buy a product or service to be part of this fad. Wealth Builders are also thinking about how to invest in these new trends and then research the companies that provide the products and services the are behind these trends. These new products and trends are always being created and evolving, even in poor economies and poor stock markets.

The global economies are very dynamic and new companies often have amazing rates of growth. It is not uncommon for a new company in a growing industry to have profit growth in excess of 30% per year for 5 or 10 years. Older, more established companies have much lower rates of return and this is why newer companies are where your child will be able to garner greater returns. Young people are often more in tune with new trends in fashion and technology. Their knowledge of these trends and products gives them a true advantage when it comes to investing.

However, spotting hot new companies and products is only part of what is needed to invest successfully. Your child should learn as much as possible about buying and selling stocks. There are many excellent publications and books on the topic (see Appendix E). Your child should learn how to read a stock chart and learn how companies are valued so that he understands when a company is cheap and when it is expensive. Your child should also learn that most stocks follow the direction of the general stock market. The lesson is to buy when the stock market is trending up. Any particular company may have a fantastic product and strong growth but its stock may flounder if the overall stock market is not performing well. About 75% of all stocks follow the direction of the general stock market. There are countless examples of "good company, bad stock" and "bad company, good stock."

We have already covered investing in real estate. One of the reasons that real estate has been such a tremendous wealth builder for generations is because real estate employs what is known as leverage.

Leverage is defined as the action of a lever; the mechanical advantage of a lever. A lever allows one to lift or move greater weight than without a lever. Archimedes said in 220 BC "Give me a place to stand and a lever long enough and I will move the world." Andrew Carnegie said "I would rather have 1 percent of 100 people's efforts than 100 percent of my own." Both Archimedes and Carnegie are expressing the power of leverage.

The financial meaning of leverage is the ability to control large dollar amounts of an asset with a relatively small amount of money. How is this done? Usually this is accomplished by borrowing money. The typical real estate example is as follows. You may buy a $100,000 property for $100,000 cash. This property may appreciate at 5% a year going forward. The buyer sees the value of this $100,000 increase by $5,000 each year. He has received a 5% return on his initial investment of $100,000, which was the cost to purchase the house.

The same buyer could employ a different strategy. He may buy two houses that each cost $100,000. Since the buyer only has $100,000, he will put a $50,000 down payment on each house and borrow $100,000, $50,000 on each house, by taking out mortgages. If houses in the area appreciate by 5% each year then each house will increase in value by $5,000 or a total of $10,000. Now, $10,000 represents a 10% return on the initial $100,000 investment to buy both houses. The buyer has used leverage in this case to increase his return. If used properly (not obtaining a mortgage that is too large) leverage is a very powerful way to build wealth and has made many ordinary people rich.

The best way to employ leverage is to purchase an appreciating asset that also creates income. Your child could employ leverage by buying the most expensive house that he can afford and then using every dollar he earns to pay the mortgage and other related expenses. While this endeavor would certainly increase your child's wealth in the long run it would not be a very good way to live. A far better way to use leverage would be for your child to buy an investment property that pays for itself. As long as the rent paid by the tenants more than covers all of the expenses related to the investment property, including the mortgage, then your child has leveraged an appreciating asset that pays for itself! Your child will receive some income each month from the rental property and he will benefit from the value of real estate increasing over time.

Leverage is also present in many businesses and this is one of the reasons that businesses have created untold sums of wealth for the business owners. If your child starts a dog walking business and charges $10 a day to walk a dog then his earnings are limited by the number of hours that he can devote to walking dogs in one day. Theoretically, this limit is 24 hours but, in reality, is far less. Let's say that your child is able to walk the dogs for two neighbors. This will allow her to charge $20 per day.

Your child may decide to pay other children to walk the dogs and pay them $6 a day. Your child would keep $4 a day for every child that walks a dog for the day. If your child were to find 10 households that needed dog walking services your child would receive $40 a day instead of $20 a day. This is the leverage that Andrew Carnegie was referring to.

Financial Precision

One of the most powerful tools that your child should understand is the concept of financial precision. Financial precision is what every business, whether large or small, spends lots of time trying to achieve. Why? Because these companies know that it is critical that they be able to measure all financial aspects of their business. Businesses need to know how much money is coming from the sale of products and services and they certainly must know how much money is going to pay expenses. If they did not measure then they could not run their businesses. Your child's financial life is very similar to a small business. He has an income and he will almost certainly have expenses.

Most people apply very little financial precision to their lives. They make financial decisions based on vague ideas about how much money they keep every month and their true level of spending. Unless your child has some way to track income and expenses, he will have a hard time making proper decisions about his finances.

Financial precision is more important today than ever before. If you think back to the time of your parents and grandparents you will see that their financial lives were much simpler. There were no

401(k)s or IRAs. If you go back far enough there were no credit cards and most people did not like to borrow unless they absolutely needed the money. Your grandparents did not have to select among the dizzying array of life insurance policies that are offered today. Your parents most likely did not spend a lot of time worrying about how they would save for retirement as pension plans were more common and the solvency of Social Security was not in doubt.

Your child will face far greater complexity in his financial life than previous generations. When he is a very young adult in the workforce his financial life will be relatively simple. He will receive a paycheck with the typical items deducted from it. His expenses will be relatively simple (especially if he keeps track of them!) and he will have very few financial responsibilities. Ten years down the road your child will most likely find that his financial life has grown far more complex.

He will be receiving income from his employer and possibly income from other sources as discussed in Multiple Streams of Income. He will probably have a car loan, life insurance policy, disability insurance policy, 401(k), IRA, savings account, money market account, mortgage, home equity line of credit, mutual fund investments and many other items that he will need to know the status of.

Financial precision is critical because it will allow your child to make sound financial decisions and choices. Have you ever overheard a young couple discussing an important financial matter such as buying a house? Well, the conversation usually follows this path. "Do you think we can afford this house because I really like it?" "Well, I don't know, it seems like it might be too expensive, but I suppose if we cut back on eating out and traveling we could afford it?" "So, does that mean we can afford it?" "Sure, I guess we can afford it."

This approach is no way to go about buying a home or making any other financial decision of any importance. A young couple who has been applying financial precision to their lives will know exactly how much after tax income they have available to pay the ongoing expenses of owning a home. They will also know exactly how much money they have saved and may use for a down payment. They also will know what their future savings goals are if they buy the house and are living in it and incurring all of the related expenses. This is the only way to approach major financial decisions. Your child will need as much information as possible.

Another very important benefit that financial precision affords is that it will allow your child to take advantage of financial opportunities. If a fantastic investment comes his way, your child will not only have the savings needed to participate in the investment, he will also have a clear picture of his finances and whether or not the investment makes senses for him.

If you start your young child on the path to financial precision by having him track his income and expenses, he will get into the habit of doing so and will apply this to his ever widening financial circle as he ages. Start with a very simple method of tracking income and expenses with your young child. Do not make it very complicated or time intensive as you do not want to discourage him from undertaking this task. Your child will find this exercise fun as he sees the amount of money he has grow slowly either through income over time or investment returns.

Your Child and Retirement Plans

There are entire books written about retirement plans and retirement planning. For better or for worse, I have read most of them. In a nutshell, you should teach your child to:

Participate as soon as possible to any and all retirement plans available to him or her. Again, saving for retirement is playing the compounding game. Time is one of the critical factors. The sooner that one invests, all other things being equal, the better the future outcome.

Put as much as possible into retirement plans. The earlier a dollar is invested and the more dollars invested, the more money your child will have in the future. This can be a very hard notion to sell your "twenty something" who feels that he should be living it up as a young person. Contributing to retirements pans is in the "pay yourself first category."

Even under the worst of circumstances, make sure that your child contributes at least as much as his employer matches. For example, if your son's employer matches 401(k) contributions at a 5%

rate then your son should at minimum contribute 5% of his paycheck each year to the 401(k) plan. Who wouldn't want a 5% raise? Well, this is exactly what the employer's 5% match is.

It is far, far easier to contribute to retirement plans early in life, even while your son's income may not be great, than it is later in life. As your child approaches his thirties and forties, it may become more difficult to contribute to retirement plans as other financial obligations come to the fore. Teach your son that starting now is the best time to begin. Maybe he will get lucky and will have so much money in his retirement plans that at the age of forty five he can stop contributing altogether! Even if this is not the case if your child gets into the habit of contributing to retirement plans early in life he is much more likely to keep contributing in the future even when money gets tight.

Have your child select a well diversified equity investment within his retirement plan. Many financial planners argue that workers in their twenties should have their retirement funds 100% in equities. Far too many young people, especially young women, choose investments that are far too conservative. It makes no sense to have 401(k) funds in a money market account for someone who is 25. This individual will have 30 or 40 years to invest and needs to take advantage of the greater return that the stock market offers. Make sure that your child begins with a broadly diversified mutual fund or index fund. Down the road he may invest in more specialized funds such as Real Estate Investment Trusts or sector funds.

Once money is put into a plan never, ever, ever take money out of a retirement plan early. If your child does so, he will have to pay Federal and State taxes along with a 10% Federal penalty for withdrawing the money before the allowed age of 59 ½. To show how damaging early withdrawals from a retirement account can be consider the following example:

Larry, who is almost 30 years old, has been diligently contributing to his employer's 401(k) plan since the age of 22. Larry has had to make sacrifices, but he was able to contribute 13% of his $50,000 salary each year. Larry's employer matches contributions at a 5% rate. Larry has $97,205 in his 401(k) plan since the plan has returned 10% a year since he began contributing. Larry decides to have a mid-life crisis and take a $10,000 vacation around the world for two weeks. In order to have $10,000 after taxes and penalties, Larry will need to withdraw $17,550. Larry takes a trip around the world for two weeks and then returns to work.

Thirty five years later, at the age of 65, the $17,550 that Larry used for his vacation would have been worth $493,198 had he left it in his 401(k) plan at a 10% annual return. This is a tremendous difference.

Never, ever, ever withdraw money from a retirement plan. There are certain exceptions for withdrawal that allow one to avoid the 10% penalty, such as buying a first home, but it still does not make sense to pull money out of a retirement plan prematurely. Many financial planners are also against borrowing from a retirement plan due to the adverse tax treatment. Enough said.

If your child is lucky enough to work for an employer that offers a 401(k) or similar plan, such as the 403(b), he should contribute from the moment he is eligible and should contribute as much as possible. Generally, contributing in incrementally greater amounts works best when young people start working. Your son should contribute at least as much as the employer will match. Then, he should try to contribute an increasing amount of money each month while getting used to the smaller paycheck as there will be less money leftover after contributing more to a retirement plan. Since the 401(k) contribution is taken out of your son's paycheck it is a great way to force savings. It is impossible to spend money that never even passes through your hands. The key is to have your son increase his weekly, or bi-weekly or monthly, depending on the plan, contributions by small amounts, say $25 or $50, so that he can adjust to having less in his paycheck.

Your son may think that he is off the hook once he has contributed to his employer's 401(k). Well, the complex retirement plan and tax rules don't make it nearly that easy. If your child is earning more than $165,000, after his 401(k) contribution, then this actually may be the end of the story. If your child is earning at this level or greater and is contributing the maximum allowed by the IRS to his 401(k) plan (have your son check with employer as to what the maximum contribution as it tends to go up each year and may even vary by company), then he may want to consider also contributing to a Traditional IRA. The only advantage to doing so is that he contributes more money to retirement, which is a good thing. However, any Traditional IRA contribution he makes is not deductible for income tax purposes because his income is too high. The income level will be indexed for inflation in future years so please check the current level.

If your child is earning less than $100,000 and is not yet married, then the situation is a little more complex. He will be eligible to contribute to a Roth IRA. For incomes between $100,000 and $165,000 a contribution to a Roth IRA is allowed but the amount is limited.

One contributes to a Roth IRA by funding it with after tax dollars. A Traditional IRA is funded with before tax dollars. The great advantage of a Roth IRA is that once the post tax dollars are placed in the IRA they grow tax free. No Federal tax is ever due. When money is withdrawn from a Traditional IRA after the age of 59 ½, it is treated as taxable income.

Now, much has been written on whether one should contribute to a Traditional IRA or a Roth IRA. Most analysis focuses on the tax bracket your son is in today compared to what bracket he expects to be in during his retirement. There are, however, many other considerations, such as estate planning benefits (yes, I am really talking about your child's estate and no I have not, yet, gone crazy!) and no requirement to start taking distributions from the Roth IRA at age 70 ½, which is a requirement for the Traditional IRA. The final thing to think about is whether tax rates will be higher or lower in 20, 30, 40 or 50 years. No one really knows so the Roth IRA, with its tax free income to your son, may be a great way to hedge against future tax uncertainty.

Many financial experts believe that tax rates will be higher than they are today in the decades to come. The increasing obligation from Social Security, Medicare and Medicaid will almost certainly require higher tax rates. If the United States decides to adopt some form of national healthcare then tax rates would be pushed even higher. Consult your financial planner for your son's specific situation and he or she should be able to guide you best in this area.

One of the biggest mistakes that young people make, other than not contributing to retirement plans at all or contributing too little, is to select investment choices that are far too conservative. Your child will have a tremendous amount of time before he will need the money from these retirement plans. Since this is the case, it usually makes the most sense to select the investments that will provide the highest return over time. This usually turns out to be a stock, sometimes called an equity, mutual fund. Do not let your son or daughter invest a significant portion of their retirement funds in money market funds, bonds or other "safe" investments. The difference between a 5% return per year and a 10% return per year over 30 years on $10,000 invested today is $131,275!

Make sure that when your child is considering moving from one employer to another that the impact on his retirement plans is part of the consideration. For example, sometimes the match that we have been discussing vests over a period of years and your son may be leaving for a new job that pays $3,000 more a year but he will be losing $6,000 worth of employer match at his current job. It makes sense to check these things out first rather than learn about them too late. I worked with a woman who left for a new job and she was going to be earning $7,000 more a year. This is a significant amount of money. However, she did not make a wise move as if she had stayed with her old employer for another three weeks, she would have realized $18,000 more in vested matching from the employer. I think she would have waited the three weeks had she realized this subtle point. In 35 years that $18,000 will be worth $505,844 at a 10% annual return!

Contributing to a retirement plan is so important that you should consider, assuming you are doing all you can for your own retirement, matching your child's retirement plan contributions to get him to put more into the plan. For example, say your child is contributing $4,000 a year to his 401(k) at work and the employer is contributing $1,750 a year for a total of $5,750. This is a nice start for a young person. However, if he could contribute just $1,000 or $2,000 more per year, the difference in terms of future value is tremendous.

Let's look at a short example. If you were to give your child $1,000 for only one year so that he could contribute another $1,000 to his retirement plan ($5,000 instead of $4,000) that extra $1,000 would be worth $17,449 in 30 years at 10% per year. If you were to do this every year for 5 years for your child, he would have $72,761 in 30 years. Since you are giving him the $1,000 he is no worse off today by putting another $1,000 in his retirement plan.

Whether your child contributes to a Roth or a Traditional IRA he should get on an automatic investment plan. For example, many brokerage firms that offer IRA plans have an automatic monthly contribution plan. If your child decides to contribute $1,500 to a Roth IRA the brokerage firm will allow him to sign up for a plan where your child will have $150 automatically taken from his checking account each month. The $150 should be taken as soon as possible after your child's paycheck for the month is in his checking account.

This is the best way to save, as we have said time and time again, as your child won't have a chance to spend this money. It is quickly transferred to your child's Roth IRA where he, hopefully, won't spend it.

Never Buy Depreciating Assets on Credit or with Equity

Never, ever, ever let your children buy depreciating assets on credit. Don't let them do it even if the rate offered is 0%. The rule is simple. If you don't have the cash today, don't buy the item. Continue to save and when you do have the cash, then you may buy the item.

Notice that I said "cash" and not "money." Your children should have the cash, in some liquid form as in a savings account, before they make a purchase. This is an important distinction. Too many young people have said to themselves, 'Well, I have no money in the bank, but my car is worth $6,000 or I have $10,000 of equity in my condo so I really do have the money." This young person is thinking of equity. Never, ever, ever spend equity to buy depreciating assets. Only spend cash.

I cannot emphasize this point enough. Many people struggle financially today because they overspend and not because of something that is beyond their control.

About Credit Cards

It used to be that credit card companies would only extend a credit card to someone who was working and could prove that they had a relatively steady income. In the 1980s a trend began where these companies were actively marketing credit cards to students in college. The companies made it very easy for students to sign up for these credit cards. When college classes would begin each semester the credit card companies had large, inviting tables set up where all a student had to do was complete an application with his name, address, telephone number and social security number. Six to eight weeks later the credit card would arrive in the mail.

I watched many of my peers in college go out and spend thousands of dollars on these credit cards over the course of a year. Some of these students ended their four year college stint with a credit card balance that was greater than most starting salaries for graduates. In many cases, the parents had no idea that their son or daughter had obtained a credit card. In a few cases, before the law was changed to make this far more difficult, these students had to declare bankruptcy to clear themselves of this debt.

Whoever "invented" credit and the credit card really understood human nature extremely well. Most people cannot help buying something they want even if they do not have the money today. They somehow rationalize that they will have the money in the future. Many young people don't even understand the concept of a credit card's "minimum payment" and that $100 charged today on a credit card will grow to several hundred dollars in the future if only the minimum payment is made. According to Cardweb.com there are more than 115 million Americans who carry monthly credit card debt, with the average being around $9,000.

Here is an example from LendingTree.com's website:

"Say your credit card company sets your minimum payment at 4 percent of your total balance, and your balance is $1,000. If you pay just your minimum payment, at 15 percent annual interest, it would take you six years and eight months to reach a zero balance. You'd also have paid almost $400 in finance charges. And that is assuming that you don't use your credit card for any additional purchases."

Make sure that you sit down with your child and explain what a credit card is and how it works. Show them that if they do not pay their balance off in full each month, the credit card company's minimum payment will pay mostly interest and hardly reduce the principal amount due. This is why it takes so long to pay off the balance. Each minimum payment does very little to pay off the loan, it just pays interest.

Teach your child that the credit card companies are very smart and they know how to make money, which costs the users of these credit cards money. Have your child read the fine print that comes with any credit card agreement. Make sure that he gets in the habit of never agreeing to or signing anything that he does not understand. In the case of a lengthy credit card agreement, it will be best for your child if he just stays away from credit cards entirely. They should only be used for emergencies or to purchase a big ticket item that your child has already saved for and has the money on hand to pay the credit card bill when it arrives.

Your Child's Credit Score

Whether we like it or not a credit score is a very important number that will affect our financial well being in the future. If you never need to borrow money then you probably do not care about your credit score. This is not the case for most people. Most of us will need to borrow money for school, for a car, for a home and maybe to buy a business. Most people don't know what their credit score is and when they do find out, it is usually too late. It is very common for people to apply for a mortgage or a car loan and assume that their credit score is good only to have the potential lender tell them that their credit score is not good. If your credit score is poor the best outcome is that you'll be able to borrow the money, but at a higher rate. The worst outcome is that you will not be able to borrow at all.

Don't ever assume that the credit scoring companies have your information represented correctly. Even if you have a fantastic credit history if the credit scoring companies do not have this information straight it will usually hurt you. Here is an interesting story about my first foray into checking my credit history.

I was twenty three years old at the time and decided to check my credit history. I wrote away to the major providers of credit histories, Equifax and TransUnion at the time. Several weeks later, I received my credit information. At the time my financial life was very simple. I was living at my parent's home, did not have a car and had borrowed no money for anything. I was working at my first job after college. It didn't take me long to see several things wrong on my credit report.

The most glaring, was a mortgage that the credit rating company had me taking out two years after I was born! The credit report had my date of birth listed correctly on the front page. At the same time, it showed me taking a mortgage out two years later. My father and I have the same first and last names and the same middle initial. Of course, we have different social security numbers. The credit rating company had mistakenly placed my father's mortgage, when he bought our family's house, on my credit report. I also found duplicate entries for a credit card and some information that had nothing to do with me.

Having a strong credit score is a real asset in life. It will allow your child to borrow when he wants at a rate that is favorable and that will save him money. Credit scores are also being looked at closely by prospective employers when they are looking to hire a candidate. There are many candidates who would have been perfect for a particular job and passed all of the requirements but were denied the job because they had a poor credit score. This thinking is catching on. Employers feel that if someone is responsible with their personal finances they will be responsible as an employee and vice versa.

I am sure that your child, whether he is at this age now or will be in the future, does not need another job in life. Unfortunately, he should check his credit history from time to time to see what his score is. The score ranges from 300 to 850 with a higher score being better. This is known as a FICO score. Scores over 720 are considered excellent and entitle the borrower to the best rates available. Scores between 680 and 700 are good and will entitle one to the typical loan rate. Scores from 620 to 680 are considered to be fine and will allow the borrower to obtain a loan but not at the most favorable terms. Scores between 580 and 620 are considered poor credit and subject the borrower to higher rates.

If the topic of credit history and scores is particularly important to your child I recommend that you do further research as there are many details that we are not able to cover here. In a nutshell, the most important factors in determining your child's credit score will be payment history, time, outstanding balance and outstanding credit.

Payment History is the record of your child's history of paying his bills. Impress upon your child that he must pay all bills on time and never late. This is one of the best ways to build a strong credit score.

Time is the amount of time that your child has had access to credit. The credit rating agencies know that there is a very big difference between someone who has been paying their bills on time for three months and someone who has been paying their bills on time for ten years. Time is a very, very important factor in your child's credit score. There is not much that your child can do about time except to make sure to use any credit he or she has during this period wisely by paying all bills on time.

Outstanding balance is the total amount of all outstanding debt, usually in relation to income. Since your child will not carry any credit card debt, the only outstanding balances that he or she should have are for the purchase of a home, an investment property or properties and to finance the purchase of a car. Credit scoring companies do not like to see very high outstanding loan amounts relative to income. Even if your child has an excellent credit score and credit history, it makes credit scoring companies nervous if he has too much debt relative to income. Ironically, the credit scoring companies do not take into account assets. They don't care if your child has $10 million in the bank as they primarily care about his income. Even if your child's income is high relative to his outstanding debt, the credit scoring companies have averages, by region, by debt level and if your child is well above these averages, his credit score will suffer.

Outstanding credit is the amount of all credit lines in total, usually compared to monthly and yearly income. Even if your child gets high marks in the other categories of payment history, time and outstanding balance, if the total amount of debt that your child has access too is very high, his credit score will suffer. Having outstanding credit that is too high is usually due to owning too many credit cards, having access to too many home equity lines of credit (we'll talk about this under home ownership) or some access line that can be drawn on from time to time. Your child should always establish, but never use except in the case of an emergency, his home equity line of credit. However, your child should ensure that he does not have too many credit cards. It is far too easy, over the years, to open up various credit cards and store credit cards because they offer some deal.

I had opened many credit cards over the years because the department store offered a special deal, such as "Get Two for the Price of One" if you opened a credit card at their store. Then, I never used that credit card again. Over time, my credit score was slowly getting worse due to all of these cards. The credit scoring companies were worried that I was going to get up one morning and buy as much as I could with all of my available credit. The solution to this problem was simple.

I wrote to the credit scoring companies and the company issuing the credit card, after cutting up these unneeded cards, and stated that I had destroyed the card and I asked them to remove these items from my credit history. Over the next six months my credit score improved.

Be warned that if your child is carrying a balance and begins to close unused credit cards his credit score could suffer. How is this possible? The credit scoring agencies look at the ratio of outstanding balance to total available credit. If your child has a $5,000 outstanding balance but has access to $25,000 of credit his ratio is 1/5. If he closes three credit cards and only has access to $10,000 worth of credit then his ratio becomes ½ and credit scoring agencies do not like to see such a high ratio. It is a strange way to look at the situation but it is what it is.

It is especially important that your child check his credit score and history well before he applies for a loan or mortgage of any kind. It takes the credit scoring companies a long time to fix errors, so it is wise to start this process six to twelve months before your child will need to borrow.

Hopefully your child has a good credit score and a favorable credit history. There are two other possibilities. He could have a poor credit or he could potentially have no credit history and this could lead to a poor credit score. It is ironic, but if someone never borrows money, pays all of his bills on time and has a lot of money in the bank he will have no credit history and very well may not be able to obtain a loan. What a great system!

Poor Credit History or No Credit History

Whether your child has a poor credit score or no credit history, there are several things that can be done to remedy the situation. Keep in mind that this remedy will take time. Usually, it takes six months to one year to either fix a bad credit score or to establish a credit history. There are many companies that will help your child better his credit score and fix his poor credit history. Some of these companies are a bit unscrupulous and some are outright frauds. I don't really see the value they provide when your child can correct his own poor credit score.

If your child just needs to start a credit history, there are several things that you may do to help him. The easiest and fastest way to help your child start building a credit history is to add him to one of your existing credit cards. Of course, you have to ensure that the payment history on this credit card is flawless. You want to help your child build his credit history and in order to do this the credit card will need to be paid on time.

You don't have to actually give your child a credit card when he is on your account, but for children who are mature this is a great opportunity to learn. As long as he only spends money that he intended to spend anyway and has the cash reserves to back the purchase there is no problem.

If you are looking to have your child establish a credit history independent of your credit history then you will have to take another approach. One way to go about this is to help your child obtain a credit card on his own. This should not be too hard these days as the credit card companies seem to issue cards to everyone. If your child has trouble obtaining a credit card there are two things that can be done to help him.

First, you may cosign the application for his credit card. While this may be the fastest way for your child to obtain a credit card, it is best if he obtain the card on his own without your name and social security number being associated with his credit card and credit history.

The second way for your child to obtain a credit card if he is having difficulty is for him to back the credit card with a bank account. Your child should already have a savings account and perhaps a checking account at this time. The credit card companies are usually happy to issue a credit card with a small limit, say $500, if they can see a bank account with $700 or more in it.

Once your child has this credit card, he would make small purchases on the card and pay the balance off as soon as it is due. Usually, your child will only use his credit card for emergencies as we have stated earlier. However, he will need to use his credit card in this case to build a credit history. The purchases that your child makes on his credit card should be things that he would usually buy and pay in cash. You may also have your child buy some bigger ticket items that your household needs. You may then reimburse him for the amount spent on the credit card. Please keep in mind the gift tax limit of $12,000 (for 2007).

This steady record of using a credit card and paying off the balance immediately will build a favorable credit history. Once this history is established, your child will be able to obtain a regular credit card without the need to back it with a savings account.

If your child has poor credit, the task may be more difficult. If the reason for the poor credit is due to credit cards with balances where your child is paying only the minimum, or less, the best way for him to improve his credit score is to start paying more than the minimum monthly payment and begin to pay down the outstanding balance more quickly. As this process occurs, his credit score will improve.

If your child has poor credit because he or she has missed payments and sometimes not paid debts, then the path is clear. A regular payment history needs to be established. Your child will need to pay down these balances over time. The balances do not need to be paid off entirely, but generally more than the minimum payment will need to be made against each balance to show the credit rating company that your child is serious about improving his credit. If multiple credit cards are involved always make the minimum payment on all of the credit cards and then apply any additional funds to the card with the highest interest rate irrespective of how large the balance is. Once the highest interest credit card is paid off concentrate on paying off the credit card with the second highest interest rate.

The Family Business

If you or someone you know has a family business you have a fantastic opportunity to expose your child to many of life's lessons that are usually not learned by most until much later in life. By working in a family business your child will be exposed to money, the need to make customers happy, the need for hard work and the need for discipline. Many people who have started businesses or come very far in the business world did not have degrees from top schools or lots of education. In many cases these business leaders were exposed to business early in life and gained experience while they were still children and young adults.

Even young children are able to help in a family business by sweeping the floors, filing or sorting mail. When a child is young it is not very important what job he does but it is very important that he has a job that he is able to do and is expected to do. Your child will derive pleasure form helping out and he will certainly enjoy being paid. As your child grows he will be able to take on more complicated tasks and will be able to contribute to a greater degree. You will be able to discuss this work with your child and find out what he thinks about work and his particular job. Teach your child that his worth to the company is directly proportional to the value that he creates for the company. The value created is what creates differences in pay within companies.

In addition to these benefits you have an opportunity to increase your child's wealth by having them involved in a family business. While you must abide by your state's labor laws your child is eligible to be paid for work done in any business. This income will allow your child to save and will make him eligible to contribute to a Roth IRA. This is a very powerful way for your child to build his wealth.

Speak to your accountant to make sure that you have addressed all of the requirements in having your child on the payroll.

Investing With Your Younger Child

When your child is old enough to understand the concept of a bank and depositing money at a bank so that it will earn interest, you should open a Custodial Money Market Account for him. This account will have your name and his name on it, but the account will be for the benefit for your child. When he turns eighteen, the money will be his as well so you'll have some time to teach him well so that he doesn't run out and spend it all.

Usually, children around the age of ten are ready for such an account. This account will be funded by the 50% of your child's income that does not go into the Savings Box. The half that your child deposits in his local bank will be his and he can use it as he sees fit.

You'll want to select an interest bearing account, such as a Money Market, where your child can deposit money whenever he pleases and withdraw money whenever he pleases. He will see that the account earns interest over time.

Make sure that your child is responsible for the account. Let him have the passbook and let him fill out the deposit slips and hand them to the teller at the bank. This will be a wonderful experience for him and it will make him feel comfortable with bank.

You will be amazed how quickly your child takes to this new responsibility. It is usually very easy to get children this age interested in going to the bank to deposit money because they feel grown up doing it.

During this period of time that your child has his own savings account teach him what a bank is and why banks exist. Sometimes, drawing pictures will help with children of this age.

Children should learn that a bank is in the business of borrowing and lending money. They should become familiar with the terms, "borrowing," "lending," "borrower" and "lender." It is always best to relate these terms to something that your child understands. If they have been involved in some of the Kid Friendly Businesses we discuss, then it will be much easier.

If your child likes to run a lemonade stand from time to time then he should understand the concept of selling lemonade in order to make a profit. Unfortunately, most parents only teach their children the revenue side of this business. In other words, the parents provide the water, lemons, sugar and ice at no charge. Your child should learn that there are costs associated with any business and a bank will lend the prepared business owner the money needed to start a business that has a good chance of succeeding. In very simple terms, the bank would lend someone the money to buy all of the items needed to setup a lemonade stand and go into business.

Children seem to usually have a hard time grasping the concept of lending and borrowing and interest is even more difficult for them to visualize. Keep exposing your child to these ideas and eventually they will "get it" and will become very smart with these concepts.

Make it a point to show your child the interest she receives in her bank account. To make this interest real rather than just a number in her passbook, it is a good exercise to have her withdraw the amount of the last interest credited to her account. This is usually a very small sum, but you should either make a small frame and paste this interest money there or use the interest money to buy something that your child wants or pay for a portion of something that she wants. She will need to actually see the money to understand that it can make a difference in her life. Continue to do this from time to time along with teaching her the lesson that she is earning this interest on the money she has deposited at the bank because the bank is "putting her money to work" by prudently lending it out to others who will use the money to start or expand businesses or need the money to finance the purchase of something, such as a car.

Investing With Your Older Child

Once your child reaches the age of eighteen, he may open his own brokerage account. Even before this time, you may open an account for your child's benefit (see the UTMA/UGMA section) and invest. Such an account will allow your child to invest in stocks and mutual funds.

When I was in college my parents bought a few stocks for me and let me review the brokerage account and check the prices from time to time. I was immediately hooked. This was a fantastic lesson for me and I was really taken by the notion that money can work for you and make more money. I think that I felt this way because at that time I was earning most of my money by caddying at a local golf course. This was the good "old fashioned" kind of caddying where the caddy carried two golf bags, one on each shoulder, through all eighteen holes of the golf course. The whole trip, or "loop" as caddies called it, took anywhere from three to five hours. This was no small feat for someone like me, who weighed one hundred and thirty pounds when some golf bags could weigh as much as forty pounds!

The fact that an investment in a stock or a money market account could yield $100 after a period of time was very exciting to me. I used to have to work very hard at the country club to make $100 and I could earn the same $100 by investing wisely and being patient. I think that your child will experience the same level of excitement and hopefully will begin a lifelong interest in investing.

Since it appears that children today are more advanced than my generation (please don't actually tell them this!) you probably can start this exercise when your child is in high school. It is very important that you let them follow the stocks for a period of many, many years as stocks go up and they go down in the short run, but history shows us that over longer periods of time they do go up. You don't want your child to get discouraged by seeing his stocks go down.

UTMAs and UGMAs – Getting the Best Deal

The Uniform Gift to Minors Act (UGMA) came into law first. The Uniform Transfer to Minors Act (UTMA) expands the previous law. Most states have adopted the UTMA which replaces the UGMA. Check in your state which type of account you'll need to open. Your child will need to have a social security number in order for an account to be established. You, or another adult, will act on your child's behalf until he reaches the age of majority in your state.

These are custodial accounts. Your name is on the account along with your child's name. You "control" the account until your child reaches the "age of majority" in your state. This is usually 18 or 21. Check your local state laws.

Once your child reaches the age of majority the money is hers to spend as she sees fit, so make sure she has learned all of the important money lessons before that time comes. Remember, the custodial account will be funded with money from the Savings Box, which is 50% of your child's earnings. This money is never to be touched and is designated to grow your child's wealth. This continues to be true once the money is in the custodial account. She should not touch this money. The idea is to let it grow to the sky over time. With the strategies laid out in this book, she may have a healthy sum by that time and you don't want her misusing this money.

The important point is that these accounts will allow you to invest on behalf of your child, no matter what their age, and invest in stock mutual funds. Being able to invest in stock, also known as equity, mutual funds will be key to ensuring that your child's money grows. See Appendix F for information on how to setup a UTMA or UGMA account and where you are able to do so.

You should invest the 50% that your child is putting in her Savings Box. Remember, she should not be allowed to touch the money once she drops it in the Savings Box. You will need access to the money as you will be investing it from time to time for her. When the amount in her Savings Box reaches $50 to $100, you should make a deposit to her custodial account. In an ideal world, any money that your child places in the Savings Box would immediately go into the custodial account to take advantage of as much time and as much compounding as possible. Then, of course, there is the practical, real world. You'll find a balance that works for you.

As mentioned previously, you really want to make sure that your daughter's money within the custodial account is invested in a stock mutual fund. Many financial advisors recommend one growth fund and one value fund, each representing half of the account's value. Other advisors recommend an index fund for all of the funds or a portion of the funds along with a growth fund and a value fund. What is most important is that you start today and not procrastinate in setting up the custodial account and contributing to it on a regular basis.

Don't make the mistake of buying savings bonds for your child or putting her money into a savings account or CD. The reason not to do is very simple. These are safe investments that have very low yields. Your child does not need safety. Your child needs maximum growth.

Your child is never supposed to touch this money, so it does not need to be in a safe investment. Money is placed in safe investments when there is an expectation that it will be needed in the near future. One example is that of retirement planning. As people approach retirement, they begin to shift money out of the stock market and into fixed income producing assets. This is a smart strategy. When you stop working you must rely on a steady stream of income that does not vary. This is what savings bonds, bonds, money market accounts and CDs provide. Your child does not need this safety. Your child needs maximum growth over the long term and this means investing in the broad stock market via mutual funds. What's the big deal you may ask? Here is a comparison. Below, is $100 invested today at several different interest rates over various time horizons.

$100 invested:

Years	4%	8%	12%
10	$148	$216	$311
20	$219	$466	$965
30	$324	$1,006	$2,996
40	$480	$2,172	$9,305

    Take a moment to look at the above chart and you are able to see how powerful the compounding effect can be. As the number of years invested increases the initial investment truly grows in size. The interest rate at which the money grows is a critical factor. Over long periods of time there is a very large difference in the end result between receiving 8% per year versus 12% per year. Your child would have $9,305 after 40 years of growth at 12% per year. This is more than 4 times the amount of $2,172 your child would have after 40 years of growth at 8%!

    Because the rate of return makes such a huge difference and your child has a long time to invest you need to make sure that your child's investments are not too safe. The younger your child is the more important it is that his investments take on some risk to achieve greater return.

    Should your child receive monetary gifts in the form of savings bonds you should thank the one giving the generous gift. Make sure to cash in these savings bonds and invest them for your child more aggressively. A child who is 3 years old does not need the safety of a savings bond or some other safe, fixed income investment.

The Dangers of Your Child Having Money

Contributing to a custodial account is sometimes the easy part. The hard part is making sure that your child has the maturity and the financial knowledge to avoid running out and spending all of your hard earned money on something that, in the long run, turns out to be silly.

Many parents who contribute to custodial accounts for their child do so without letting the child know that she has this money in her name. This approach tends to make sense. It allows the child to focus on saving her own money and building her wealth rather than sitting around and waiting for money to come her way. Nothing seems to sap motivation more than a child knowing that money will eventually fall into his or her lap. Why work today when there is a payday in the future?

Many parents have the account statements sent to a relative or to their place of work so that the child does not see the statements in the mail and potentially open the envelope. This strategy works until the child becomes involved in preparing their own income taxes (unless the money is in an IRA, preferably a Roth IRA!), which usually happens around the age of twenty one, give or take a year so. This is when parents have to make hard choices and have a discussion with their child.

Some children will be more mature in this area than others. Hopefully, Wealthy Child has created an understanding in your child of money and the importance of letting money grow. If this is not the case, then your job will be more difficult. The custodial account will give your child full access to the money once she reaches the age of majority in your state. There is little stopping them from pulling the money out of the account. I have known parents who have threatened to give the money away to charity before the child has access to the money.

The best way to ensure that you do not wind up in this situation is to teach your children early on about the importance of money and of compounding. If they are just able to see the power of keeping the money and letting it grow, they usually will be excited about the prospects. If your child is considering taking the money and running once they are old enough, sit down with her and explain how this money can grow. If all else fails, ask your child to make you a promise that they won't touch the money until they are 40 years old. By the time your child reaches this age she won't want to touch the money and may be thinking about passing money along to her child or children! Remember, this is your money since you gave it to your child in the first place.

For each $1,000 she has in her custodial account at the age of eighteen, she could see many times this amount in the years to come. At 10%, the growth would be as follows:

Age:	Amount:
30	$3,138
35	$5,054
40	$8,140
45	$13,110
50	$21,114

If she has $5,000 in her account and is able to achieve a 15% annualized return in a good mutual fund, then she'll have $26,751 when she is thirty and $437,825 at the age of fifty.

The Worker and the Capitalist

When I was growing up, my friends and I were taught by our parents that we needed to study hard, do our homework and do well in school so that we would get good jobs when we were older. This is very important advice and the alternative to following this advice is not very appealing. It was only later in life that I realized that my parents had only taught me half the rules needed to play this game we call "personal finance." It was even later that I learned that while my parents were teaching me how to obtain a "good job" by working hard in school, the people from rich families, that I was to meet later in life, were being taught the half I learned ***plus*** the other half.

I was taught to be a worker. My friends from rich families were taught to be capitalists. There is a very big difference. A worker's primary financial asset, especially in the early years, is his own body and mind. Whether that worker digs ditches, performs brain surgery or argues cases in a court of law he or she is still a laborer because money is earned "by the hour." If an hour of work is not performed then no pay is realized. As we have discussed, work is good for your child's development, it builds character and can lead to great personal satisfaction, but work in a productive career should be supplemented with a healthy dose of capitalism.

My wealthy friends had gone to the same colleges and graduate schools that my, for lack of a better term, "poor" friends had attended. These wealthy friends also worked hard to obtain jobs that paid well. They worked hard in those jobs and sought to increase their income by providing value for their employers. But, there was a big difference between "them" and "us." We all were earning the same salary, let's call it $X per year. However, my wealthy friends were also earning another $X, or sometimes $2X or $3X, from their invested capital. One friend owned a portion of a business. Another wealthy friend owned a fair number of investment properties. These friends had not been given these businesses or investment properties by their parents. However, their parents had taught them to think and act like capitalists. While I was busy working and saving my money in a bank account, my wealthier friends were looking for ways to smartly invest their money so that it would become working capital that would produce a stream of income. They had been taught the Fifth Pillar of Wealth, Wealth Building.

Building wealth is what your child should focus on as he begins to master earning, saving and investing. Most people think that investing is building wealth and that is certainly a part of wealth building, but only one part.

The largest past of The Fifth Pillar is best described as a mindset. It is a way of thinking that always pays attention to the changes in our world and constantly seeks opportunity. We all know someone like this. Sometimes, we think people like this are lucky or that they are "born with it." While I am sure that luck and heredity play a part in this skill, I have seen, firsthand, that by far the most important element is practice. Just like ice skating, reading or speaking a foreign language, practice will make your child better at nearly everything he does.

So, how do we get our children to think like Wealth Builders? By mastering the first three Pillars they are well on their way to wealth building. They have a tremendous advantage over other people because they are more conscious of money and investing issues. Most people will spend more time in one year hunting for bargains at the grocery store than they will analyzing their finances and making thoughtful investment decisions. Your child will have a healthy relationship with money and will spend time thinking about how to better his financial position. It is this level of awareness that will allow your child to take advantage of opportunities.

Instill this thought process and this level of awareness in your child and then encourage them to follow Pillar Five: Wealth Building. It is these methods that will truly propel your child into the financial stratosphere and hopefully will lead them to financial independence in the future. Once you child reaches financial independence, defined as being able to pay all ongoing living expenses from recurring, passive income, he or she will have freedom and flexibility in life to follow hobbies, charity and dreams.

The Money Game

The Money Game does not require that you buy a board game or software for your PC. The Money Game is simply taking everyday life and making it an opportunity for your child to learn. You certainly already know that children are inherently very curious and want to see how things work. They also want to be involved in things so that they may experience how they work firsthand. You have countless opportunities in any given week to teach your child about money and its function in everyday life. Make these opportunities fun for your child and he will learn quickly.

If you sit back and think about all of the financial transactions you are involved in during one month you will surely see plenty of opportunities to involve your child in some of them. For young children the best opportunities are exposing them to the cost of things and relating dollar amounts to products. Your child will learn that a gallon of milk may cost $3.50 where you live. He can pay the cashier with a $5 bill and then you and your child can count the change to ensure that he understands the transaction. It is best to use bills and coins when teaching young children as you'll want to provide examples that are as concrete as possible. Paying an electric bill with a check and then dropping an envelope in the mailbox may be too abstract for young children. Stick to the physical, real world examples whenever possible.

As children become older you will be able to expose them to a wider range of financial concepts and transactions. They may be able to swipe your credit card at the gas station and then review the receipt with you so that they are able to understand how much a gallon of gas costs. You will have a chance to tell your child how a credit card works and that you always pay the bill in full each month to avoid paying interest. You will be able to stress that you would never spend money on the credit card that you did not already have in the bank. The credit card should not be used for borrowing it should only be used as a time saving device to make life a little easier. You should stress that sometimes people cannot handle credit cards and these people should not use credit cards and should stick to cash.

As your child continues to grow you may involve them in your family's finances if you are comfortable doing so. Theoretically, an older child would be able to participate in paying your mortgage and property taxes. They also may benefit from seeing how your family invests its money. Some parents have even made their children responsible for opening bills as they arrive in the mail, reading them, sorting them and preparing them to be paid and mailed out.

If you are affiliated with a family business you'll have even more opportunities to involve your child in the financial side of the business. Part of their paid work at the business should involve dealing with numbers whether this be paying some expenses or making deposits at the bank

The key is to make the learning process fun and realize these opportunities from time to time. You'll need to take time at these moments to help your child learn about money and how money relates to our everyday lives.

Good and Bad Debt

Let's review, once more, the difference between good debt and bad debt. Good debt and bad debt are simply extensions of the good use of money. In an ideal world people who are looking to build their wealth would never spend money on "depreciating assets" such as cars, entertainment, food, etc. This is clearly not realistic. The key is to keep such spending to a reasonable level so that there is money available to buy "appreciating assets" such as real estate, a stake in a growing business, equities, etc. This is one sure way to wealth. If $1 is "spent" today to buy an appreciating asset that is worth $1.50 in 10 years you have grown your wealth. If $1 is "spent" today on a depreciating asset and is worth 30 cents 10 years from now you have just reduced your wealth.

Recall that debt is leverage. When you borrow to buy something your return is the amplified result of the final outcome. If I put $1,000 of my own money plus $4,000 of borrowed money into an investment (a total of $5,000) that is worth $10,000 in 6 years my return is 500%, which is the $5,000 gain ($10,000 value today - $5,000 initially invested) divided by my initial out of pocket cost of $1,000.

If the same investment had soured and was worth $100 in 6 years my return is -90%.

Since debt amplifies your return it hurts more when you buy depreciating assets and helps more when you purchase appreciating assets. This is why you rarely want to buy depreciating assets with borrowed money or on credit. You will pay interest on this loan and the underlying asset will decrease in value over time.

All consumer goods lose value over time. Some examples of consumer goods are cars, TVs, stereos, computers, clothes, house furnishings, appliances, vacations, entertainment, etc. Any item that is reasonably expected to loose value over time is not an investment it is an expense.

Try to use borrowed money and credit only to buy things that will most likely increase in value over time. By borrowing money you will be able to buy more of this item that you would if you had to pay all cash using only funds that you had on hand.

Kid Friendly Businesses

In many parts of America today the world has become very competitive. This competition is evident in the workforce as employees compete for the best and highest paying jobs. A little competition is a good thing as it keeps everyone on their toes and keeps things moving. However, competition, like all things in life, can be overdone.

Excessive competition is beginning to impact some children as parents, rightly so, wish to see their children excel in school in the hopes of attending a top college or university. In addition to the need for good grades many parents feel that their child must be part of sports and other extracurricular activities. These endeavors not only help our children learn the lessons of the world but they also beef up the children's transcripts, hopefully making them more appealing to colleges.

One unintended consequence of this full schedule is that many children do not have time to take on a part time job. When I was growing up it was very common for children to work part-time and sometimes full time during the summer. Many parents today do not want their child wasting his time at a job. These parents should think twice about this line of reasoning. A part time job is a wonderful way for our children to learn the lessons of work, the workplace and the value of money. If a child has not held a job during high school or college he or she will enter the workforce without any work experience. He or she may have no idea what it is like to "earn a dollar." I strongly recommend that your child work during his teen years. Yes, his primary job is school but working, to some extent, will make him a better, smarter person.

      It is almost never too soon to expose your child to the world of business. Children should learn the basic concepts of selling, marketing and budgeting. They seem to have plenty of experience with buying merchandise so make sure they are exposed to the other side.

The perennial favorites for children are as follows:

- Lemonade Stand
- Mother's Helper
- Walk dogs / take care of pets
- Sweep outside stairs and stoops
- Cut grass (for older children)
- Pickup mail while a neighbor is away
- Water plants
- Keep an eye on a house while a neighbor is away
- Shovel snow

      This is only a small sample. There are many, many ways in which your child may earn extra money by providing a valuable service to people next door or in your neighborhood. By taking on one of these businesses your child will learn the value of money and will learn that he needs to command a certain level of discipline to meet his obligation.

      The best businesses for children in their early teens are those that require a long term commitment such as a task that must be performed a few times a week for several weeks or months. This will teach your child the true nature of work.

      Your child should learn that he is not only a worker in his business but that he is the business owner as well. He created a business out of nothing and this business is now creating income for him. He should try to grow and improve his business. He will derive a sense of satisfaction from this as the business will be his and he will run it as he sees fit.

Make sure that your child understands that it is acceptable if he makes mistakes in running his business as long as those mistakes are corrected and customers are kept happy. Mistakes are not be feared and many business ideas need to be improved and some businesses fail. If your child understands that as he gains experience he will make fewer mistakes and he will be less afraid of making mistakes.

Teach your child that running a business is hard. He should learn sooner, rather than later, that the things in life that are the most rewarding are those that are the hardest. Very few things in life are easy. Children do not seem to naturally understand this and need constant reminding.

As your child works make sure that he saves money according to the rules we have already covered. Talk to him about what he likes and dislikes about the job. Have him think about ways to do his job better and faster so that he may earn more with less effort in the future. As your child is running his own dog walking mini-empire talk to him about the companies that make the products that he likes. Help him learn about business and how companies work. It will be easier for him to understand some of these concepts since he will have the example of his own business to draw upon.

More on the Roth IRA

Since we are on the topic of your child and potential business ventures we should cover a topic that is being used by the wealthy to give their children a tremendous head start in their financial lives. They are having their children contribute money to a Roth IRA. At first glance this seems a little silly. Why does a child need a retirement plan such as an IRA? The answer is very simple. A child has decades ahead of him and any money put aside today will grow tremendously over the next 20, 30 or 40 years. Furthermore, the Roth IRA is funded with after tax dollars. Therefore, no income tax is ever due after your child turns 59 ½!

Let's think about this for a minute and look at an example. Charlie and Joey are best friends, live next door to each other and are 16 years old. They both have part time jobs during the school year and work full time during the summer. They each earn about $4,000 a year after taxes and are paid W2 wages by their employers. This is earned income in the eyes of the IRS. Charlie's father insists that Charlie contribute $4,000 to a Roth IRA. Now, Charlie's Dad knows there is no way that Charlie is going to do this on his own as that would leave Charlie with nothing left over from his original $4,000.

Charlie's father decides to work overtime throughout the year to earn an extra $4,000. He gifts this money to Charlie and then Charlie contributes this $4,000 to a Roth IRA. Joey's parents decide that Joey can wait until he is out of college and working to contribute to a retirement plan. Joey is very diligent and starts immediately at age 21 to contribute to a Roth IRA since he is working. Charlie starts working at the same time and contributes to a Roth like Joey.

At age 35, Charlie has $24,463, assuming a 10% annual return, in his Roth IRA from that single $4,000 contribution he made at age 16. Charlie is this much ahead of Joey with respect to this retirement savings. At age 40, this $24,400 has grown to $39,399. At age 65 when Charlie is ready to retire he thinks back fondly to his Dad and the fact that he contributed $4,000 to a Roth IRA at the age of 16. That original $4,000 contribution has grown to $426,876! Charlie has $426,876 more than Joey at the age of 65 because of the simple act of contributing $4,000 to a Roth IRA at age 16.

While the financial experts tell me that the IRS has not ruled one way or the other on the exact age at which a child may begin contributing to a Roth IRA (check with your advisor), let's look at another example.

If Charlie had earned income at age 5 and was able to contribute $4,000 just once to a Roth IRA his account would grow, as follows, assuming a yearly return of 10%:

Age	Amount
35	$69,798
45	$181,037
55	$469,563
65	$1,217,927
75	$3,158,988

You can see why the wealthy are big on Roth IRAs for children. For a relatively small sum (no need to start with $4,000 as even $1,000 goes a long way) contributed today their children amass a fortune over time and no tax is due once the children turn 59 ½! To learn more on the specifics you may purchase *Roth IRAs for Youngsters* by visiting www.GroWWealthy.com

Live at Home

When young people ask me for financial advice one of the first tips that I offer is that they should live at their family home as long as possible before going out on their own and renting. I can tell you that this is not very popular advice.

Many young people finish school and can't wait to get a place of their own and start living their life. This is one of life's big steps and it is exciting for your child and should be enjoyable. It is also very expensive.

It is not at all uncommon to have a young person graduate college at the age of 21 or 22 and spend the next 10 years renting. It is also far too common for young people in this situation to have no significant savings at the end of this 10 year period. The freedom of being out on your own carries a high price tag.

While your child's situation is unique and every family must decide how they will handle these issues it pays for your child to think long and hard about whether he should live at home or rent a place of his own.

As a parent you can help your child compare the option of living at home and renting a place of their own. One very big selling point is the money they will accumulate over time by living at home. Whether you decide to charge your child rent or not is up to you. Many financial experts agree that a child who lives at home should pay rent and should help around the house. I tend to agree. There is no point in trying to shelter a young adult from the real world. In any case, your child probably will pay less living at home than he would in rent for his own place. He should be able to save more money.

If your son were able to save an extra $300 a month by living at home he would have $3,600 at the end of the year. If he lived at home for 3 years before moving out on his own he would have at least $10,200 more than he would if he had rented during this period. Review specific numbers with your child. If rent would cost him $1,500 a month and he paid $500 a month to live at home he would be able to save $12,000 a year or $36,000 over 3 years! This does not include the interest earned during this time.

The other benefit to living at home is the sharing of tasks. If your son were to rent an apartment by himself he would be responsible for everything. He would have to shop for food and prepare his meals. He would have to clean the apartment from time to time. He would have to take the garbage out and change the lightbulbs. If he were to live at home he would most likely have to take care of fewer tasks. This translates into your son having more free time. This is usually a big selling point with young people.

Buy a Home as Soon as Possible

If living at home after graduation while your child is working is a big financial advantage, owning his own place early in life can be an even better way to financial well being.

When I was in my senior year of college I was desperately trying to find five other people who would agree to buy a house and split the cost of doing so six ways. I thought it was a fantastic idea as I had found a perfect house for $200,000 that was near New York City and would be an easy commute. In order to put 20% down, which is typical, on the house each of the six individuals would have had to put up about $6,700 or 1/6 of $40,000. Most of my friends had several thousand dollars from working summers and many could have made up the shortfall by borrowing from their parents. We would have had a $160,000 mortgage with each of the six individuals owing 1/6 of this or a little less than $27,000. I had an agreement drawn up that if anyone wanted to leave before four years, they would have to agree to be bought out at 75% of market rate and would have to wait one year to be paid to give the others a chance to raise the money. This was to give people an incentive to stay with the original agreement.

Unfortunately, no one else thought it was a good idea. In fact, they thought it was one of dumbest ideas that they had ever heard. I tried in vain during the last few months of our senior year to convince anyone I could that owning was much better than living at home and certainly better than renting.

I moved back in with my parents while I worked my first job and paid rent to them of $350 a month. This was a good deal at the time, but certainly not a steal. Many of my college friends, many of whom refused to go in on the house purchase, decided to rent apartments in New York City. The rents ranged from $900 to $1,700 a month.

Five years went by and many of my former college friends all got together for dinner and drinks. Even though many of them had been earning very, very good salaries, they had saved almost nothing. In addition to paying high rents, they were victims of the New York City lifestyle. This lifestyle included never cooking for oneself, eating in or out constantly, partying and going to bars several times a week. I had been able to save a significant amount of money because I had low overhead expenses as I lived with my parents. Everyone was shocked to find out that the $200,000 we considered "expensive" before graduation had appreciated to almost $400,000! That is an appreciation of nearly $200,000 or about $33,300 per person. Now, the original proposal had each of six individuals putting up about $6,700 as a down payment. At $400,000, each person's equity stake was this original $6,700 plus about $33,300 or about $40,000. This is a return of 397% on the original investment of $6,700 or about 37% a year! Granted, this was a good real estate market, but the contrast is striking. My friends after five years had accumulated no significant wealth. Had we all bought the house, we would have each been $33,300 wealthier. Fast forward ten years, that $40,000 would be worth $103,750 at 10% per year. If we had kept that house, which continued to appreciate at about 7% a year, each person's equity would have amounted to $78,686. This would be a very large down payment on a house for each of the six participants at a time in life when they were each getting married, having children and looking for a house of their own.

While you should check the historical rate of return from owning a house in your area, and it will probably be around 5 to 6% per year, real estate can be a great investment that takes advantage of leverage, shows less volatility than other investments and can be a fun way to invest.

If your child shows that he or she is financially responsible to some degree, owning a home can be a great lesson for them. Owning a first home, however modest or grand it may be, will teach your child about the expenses related to owning one's own home. Your child will learn, firsthand, about all of the little, unexpected expenses that only a homeowner can appreciate. She will learn about property taxes and how to fix things around the house or wisely pay someone else to handle these tasks.

She will also learn to budget and save for those things that we all want in our homes, but are not critical. Learning to save, and not buying on credit, for that new couch or having the house painted just because she prefers a new color are important lessons that will make her smarter about money management in the future.

One of the other important lessons your child will learn is the investment potential of real estate. While we cover some specific topics related to real estate investing later, your child will learn about leverage and some of the great tax advantages to owning a home.

If you think that your child is ready for this step, then I recommend that you help them to purchase their first home. If you were fortunate enough to have been in a position to put money away for your child when she was younger you may find that these investments have grown to a considerable sum that will help your child secure her first home.

How you go about helping your child is up to you and your family. Some families will loan the child the money and others will make an outright gift. I generally feel that children should earn their own way and should not be given handouts because I feel that this teaches the wrong lesson. I make a few exceptions to this general rule and helping your child to obtain their first home is one of these exceptions.

Owning a first home will help your child build wealth in the long run. Owning a home is a great wealth building vehicle for the following reasons:

Interest on your child's mortgage and his property taxes will usually be tax deductible. The government will actually help your child live in his own home!

Leverage. Assuming your child takes out a mortgage to own her first home, she will be using leverage to better her net worth. If she buys a $200,000 home and borrows $160,000 by getting a mortgage she has $40,000 of her own money invested in the property. Now, if real estate increases by 10% over the next two years her home will have increased in value by $20,000. This is a 50% return on her initial $40,000 investment. This is possible because your daughter is using the bank's money (the mortgage) as leverage to improve her rate of return.

Forced savings. Many people who have accumulated substantial amounts of money have done so because they have owned a home for decades. They have consistently made their mortgage payments during this time and eventually paid their mortgage off. Even before paying his mortgage off, your child will benefit because each month that your child pays his mortgage a portion of that payment goes to paying mortgage principal, which reduces the total balance. If your son owns a home that is worth $200,000 and it appreciates by 5%, he has increased his net worth by $10,000 or 5% of $200,000. During this time he may have reduced his mortgage balance by $2,000 because a portion of each monthly mortgage payment goes to principal. In total, your son is $12,000 better off at the end of the year than the beginning of the year. This forced savings makes a huge difference over time.

The opportunity to improve the value of the home through smart investing. While not all home renovation projects will yield a positive return many do. Sometimes a new siding job or having the interior painted will increase the value of the house by more than the amount invested.

Building a strong credit score. If your son pays his mortgage each month and is never late this positive payment history will improve his credit score and may make him eligible for lower rates on other loans, saving him money for many years down the road.

All of these considerations don't take into account the increase in self esteem and the sense of accomplishment that your child will experience by owning their own home. It is a rite of passage and will make your child proud that she owns her own home. It is certainly a more positive feeling than paying rent out each month and increasing her landlord's equity rather than her own.

How to Buy the Right Sized Home

I have seen many young people buy more home than they should. What does "should" mean? Well, it means that they should have bought a smaller home to be consistent with their other goals.

If your child buys a small, manageable place early in life, perhaps with your help, then he or she will at least have an idea as to how expensive a home can be. The lesson that your child will learn is that there are many hidden expenses that come with owning a home from repairs, to furnishing to the desire to improve the home. Thinking about only the mortgage and property taxes misses a large part of the overall picture.

Whether your child has owned a home before or not, your job as a parent is to ensure that your child thinks through the purchase of their "permanent home." Now, nothing is permanent like it used to be, but when your child is about to buy a home that they are likely to stay in for many years, it is very important that they buy right. This usually occurs during your child's late twenties or thirties. Once your child has finished school, has a job that is relatively stable and lives in an area he likes, he is unlikely to move. If he is married and has children, he will be even less likely to move. On average, the typical American moves every 7 years. This can be a long time in the real estate market.

Let's look at the way most first time homebuyers approach the process. They tend to ignore the price of the home. Ignore may be a strong word, but very few people pay cash for a house. They usually finance a good portion of their home purchase. Since they finance the purchase of a home with a mortgage, the purchase price is not very important to people. More important to most buyers is the monthly payment. The monthly payment on the purchase of a home will include, at the very least, the mortgage and the property taxes. How do most people decide what they are able to afford on a monthly basis? The answer is that I really don't know. I have seen people make this important decision without doing any analysis whatsoever. They simply think they can afford the monthly payments.

If they are correct and they can, then there is no problem. If they are incorrect and they cannot really afford the monthly payments the trouble begins. Owning a home should be fun. Yes, it is hard work and it is expensive, but it can be, and should be, very enjoyable. If your child buys a home that he cannot afford, the experience of owning a home, instead of being fun, will be miserable. The home will consume all of his money. He will have no money to furnish it the way he likes and to fix it up to make it his own. He will have no money to go out and have fun from time to time.

Let's think about the right way to go about owning a home. One thing that is very true today is that you should never, ever borrow as much as the banks will allow you to buy. I don't feel that it offers enough of a safety cushion.

The amount of money that banks will lend to you based on your income will change as the real estate market changes. Strangely enough, when the real estate market is very hot, banks will lends you too much money. This is usually when house prices are high relative to income. When the real estate market is poor, banks are very cautious and they will lend you less, relative to your income. You'll need to decide what level of borrowing makes sense for you.

In order to figure out what makes sense for your child to borrow when buying a house, he should look to the level of savings he will have if he does buy the house. For example, if he is considering buying a house that will entail a monthly mortgage payment of $1,200 and property taxes of $300 a month, how will he know if he can afford this house?

He should first ask himself how much of his income does he want to save. Is it 10%, 12% or 20%? If your child's income at the time is $50,000, he'll have about $34,000 after taxes. At $1,500 a month for the mortgage and the property tax, he'll have $16,000 leftover. Now, there will be utility bills, the cable bill, maintenance around the property, etc. He'll need to estimate these by talking to other homeowners. Let's say all of these expenses come to $6,000 a year or $500 a month. The $16,000 becomes $10,000. $10,000 is 20% of $50,000. Now, we know that your son will use some of his $10,000 to have fun and take trips, etc. But, the conclusion is that your son is able to afford this house.

The approach should be to determine what percentage of his income your son wants to save first and then see if he can maintain that level of savings after buying and living in the house. This is the best way to approach buying a home.

Why not buy a smaller house and try to pay all cash for it? This could be done and many people, who are lucky enough to have the cash, do exactly this. However, if your child is responsible, having a mortgage will increase his net worth. While there are many different opinions on whether a mortgage is a good or a bad thing one thing we do know is that, if used properly, a mortgage can improve one's net worth substantially through the use of leverage. It is not always wise to buy the smallest and/or cheapest house.

Let's take two brothers, Larry and Harry, who are twins and are 30 years old. They are both looking to purchase their first home. Each has $200,000 in cash. Larry finds a house for exactly $200,000 and pays all cash. Harry finds a house down the street from Larry that costs $400,000. Harry puts a $200,000 down payment on the house, or 50%, and obtains a mortgage for $200,000.

Fast forward thirty years later when all real estate has increased ten fold during this period of time. This equals about an 8% annual return. Larry's house is worth $2 million and Harry's house is worth $4 million. This difference of $2 million illustrates the power of leverage used properly. Harry is $2 million better off than his brother Larry because Harry took a mortgage out and purchased a larger house. Of course, larger homes generally have higher expenses such as property taxes and maintenance items. Harry also had to pay mortgage interest during this period but he should still be well ahead. We have ignored these differences in our example. Many people have become wealthy by buying real estate with a mortgage and having that leverage work for them over time.

When the topic of mortgages comes up there is always a discussion on the various types of mortgages available. One of the biggest differences is that between fixed and floating rate mortgages. A fixed rate mortgage is the type that historically everyone was familiar with. You borrowed from the bank for a thirty year period at an agreed upon rate of interest that never changed. Floating rate mortgages have an interest rate that changes periodically based upon the general level of interest rates in the economy.

Which is best? As is usually the case, it depends on what you are trying to achieve. If your child is pretty sure that he will stay in his house for many years to come then a fixed rate mortgage is the way to go. Why worry about fluctuating interest rates and put your home (notice I said home and not house) at risk? There is enough to worry about today without the fear that you may lose your home one day due to higher interest rates. There are many other investment opportunities out there. There is no reason to speculate on your home by subjecting it to changing interest rates. Remember, it is your home.

Now, if the house your child lives in will soon be sold for whatever reason then a floating rate mortgage may make sense. Your child may have access to a floating rate mortgage that is much cheaper than the fixed rate options available. Let's make it easy and say that your daughter is living in a house that she knows that she will sell in four years. By taking a 5 year floating rate mortgage, she will save thousands of dollars in mortgage payments over those four years.

It is best to discuss your child's options and goals in life with a financial professional. He or she will be able to lay out various scenarios and make your child aware of all of the mortgage products available.

Another common point of discussion when it comes to fixed rate mortgages is whether a 15 year or 30 year fixed mortgage is best. Again, there is no right answer but I do think there is a smart way to approach this question.

Many proponents of 15 year mortgages have good reasons for choosing a 15 year term instead of a 30 year term. Here are a few:

- I don't want to be 58 years old and still paying a mortgage.

- I want to pay my mortgage off as fast as possible.

- I want my mortgage paid off before the kids start going to college. This way I will have some free money that used to go to paying my mortgage to help with the college bills.

- I want to own my home sooner rather than later. I don't want the bank to own any part of my home.

- Debt is bad and the sooner I get rid of my mortgage the better.

I will agree that these all can be good reasons to people. If your child finds himself interested in a 15 year fixed rate mortgage, let me make a proposal for how he should go about it.

He should consider obtaining a 30 year fixed mortgage and then pay this mortgage on a 15 year fixed rate schedule. Remember, a 15 year mortgage has a monthly mortgage payment that is just about double that of a 30 year mortgage. For many people this is why they do not choose a 15 year mortgage. It is too expensive on a monthly basis. If your child can afford the house by getting a 15 year mortgage he still should get a 30 year mortgage and pay it off like it was a 15 year mortgage.

The reason is very simple. Should your child ever get into financial trouble, such as losing his job for an extended period of time, the 30 year mortgage payment will be easier to pay out of his savings. He will be able to go longer before failing to meet his mortgage payment and potentially losing his home. This is a very important consideration. It would be a shame to be stuck to a 15 year fixed mortgage payment lose a job and then lose your house when you could have been fine with a 30 year mortgage.

Of course, the trick in following this advice is to have the discipline to pay a 30 year mortgage on a 15 year schedule. It requires a lot of discipline to pay a lot more than the bank is asking for each month. If your child has this discipline then he should pay off the 30 year mortgage on a 15 year mortgage schedule.

As long as we are talking about disaster planning for your child's house, he should obtain a home equity line of credit as soon as possible after buying his home. A home equity line of credit is like a second mortgage but your child will decide whether to tap this mortgage. The bank will give your child a checkbook. As long as no checks are written no money is borrowed from the home equity line of credit and no interest or fees are incurred. If a check is written against the home equity line of credit then your child will usually be charged the Prime Rate plus or minus some spread depending on the terms of the home equity line offer.

Having a home equity line of credit is very important in case your child needs money in a pinch. This could be for emergencies or it could be to take advantage of an opportunity. The Prime Rate plus or minus a spread is usually far lower than the rate on credit cards and usually far lower than the rate on the consumer loans. The only rate that is usually better is the rate on a primary mortgage on one's primary residence.

Your child should obtain the home equity line of credit even though he does not need the money today. Remember the old saying, "A bank will only lend you money when you don't need it." If your child lost his job and then asked the bank for money to carry him over until he found another job, the bank most likely would not lend him a nickel. If your child has a home equity line in place before losing his job, he may use it to help with his finances until he finds another job. In this case, the bank has no idea that your child is currently unemployed. They do not ask questions if your child writes a check against the home equity line of credit.

If your child does not have enough fiscal discipline to be able to keep the home equity line of credit checkbook for emergencies only then it is best that they do not obtain a home equity line of credit. For too many people, these lines of credit are simply another way to get in over their heads.

If your child has credit card debt, often at rates from 15% to 22%, and is able to obtain a home equity line then he should write checks against the home equity line to pay off the credit cards. As discussed, the rate on a home equity line is usually far lower than the rate on credit cards. The result is that your child will have a lower interest cost on the borrowed money and this will allow him to pay off the entire amount more quickly.

College

Education is by far the best way to improve one's financial situation. As the world's advanced economies progress jobs that require "thinking" and "knowledge" continue to grow at a rapid pace while jobs that require "muscle" are dwindling. In this environment the workers who have education and knowledge earn far higher wages than those who are less educated and posses less specialized knowledge. It is now more important than ever that your child obtain further education. While attending a college or a university is a fantastic way to obtain an education and greater knowledge this path is not for everyone. However, further education, in the form of a trade school or specialized training, is for everyone who wants to excel financially.

    For those who decide to attend a college or a university there is a perennial debate on the type of curriculum that should be pursued. Many feel that specialization is the key to success in today's economy. Others feel that specialization will give your child a rapid boost in earnings potential upon graduating college but that at some point earnings hit a cap. The "worker bees" usually only earn so much. The highest paid jobs in the world's economies today are those that require thinking, writing, speaking and communicating ideas. These top jobs require critical thinking and problem solving. Hence, pursuing an undergraduate degree in liberal arts, with a focus on an analytical major, appears to be a sound approach. A liberal arts degree is especially appealing if your son or daughter will go on to graduate school where they will obtain a degree with substantial analytical work.

A liberal arts education will impart these critical skills to your child. Your child will need to learn to read quickly and retain much of what he reads. A liberal arts education should stress large amounts of reading and honing the skill of retention so that your child is able to remember what he has read and relate it to other knowledge that he already has.

A liberal arts education should involve a substantial amount of writing. Communication is a very, very important part of success in any career. A large part of communication is still in the form of the written word whether in the form of a printed article or in a brief email. Your child should enroll in classes that focus on the skill of writing. Writing does not come easily to most people but continued practice is able to make a substantial difference in your child's ability to write clearly and concisely. These classes, along with others that stress reading, will be of great benefit to your child in a wide range of careers.

A liberal arts education should also stress speaking as a form of communication. While most liberal arts programs do well at providing classes that focus on reading and writing many do not specifically address speaking. Of course, participation in class usually involves speaking in some form as do group projects and presentations. However, a class in public speaking and/or debate may take your child's speaking ability to the next level. Debate and public speaking will help your child feel more comfortable while speaking in front of a large audience. Most people are not comfortable with public speaking in any form and continued practice will benefit your child greatly.

Tracking Your Net Worth

Your son or daughter should keep track of their net worth. They do not need to obsess over it but they should take stock every so often to see whether they are gaining ground financially or not. The financial precision that has been applied to your child's overall financial situation applies to his or her net worth as well.

Calculating net worth is rather straightforward. All assets should be listed and then a total created. All liabilities should be listed with a total as well. Your child's net worth is the difference between the assets and liabilities.

Let's look at the net worth of a diligent 25 year old:

Assets:

Savings Account	$3,200
Checking Account	$2,400
Money Market Account	$3,000
401(k)	$3,800

Mutual Funds	$2,300
Value of Car	$9,300
Furniture, etc.	$910

	$24,910

Liabilities:

Car Loan	$3,100
Student Loans	$8,000

	$11,100

Net Worth	$13,810

Some assets are easy to value. Bank accounts, 401(k)s, mutual fund accounts are easy to place a value on because they have an exact dollar amount. Other items, such as cars, furniture and electronics may not have an exact value. Their true value is what you would be able to sell them for. Someone who is 35 will usually have a more complicated New Worth statement:

Assets:

Value of Home	$382,000
Savings Account	$11,000
Checking Account	$9,000
Money Market Account	$15,000
401(k)	$37,300
Mutual Funds	$36,500
Value of Cars	$42,000
Furniture, etc.	$2,900

	$535,700

Liabilities:

Mortgage	$285,000
Car Loans	$33,100
Student Loans	$4,500

	$322,600

Net Worth $213,100

    Your child should update his net worth from time to time but should also keep his old net worth statements for comparison. It can sometimes be disheartening to look at one's net worth statement and feel that it is a very small number. However, it helps to look at past net worth statements to provide great satisfaction to see that your net worth is growing over time.

    Not only will a net worth statement give your child an idea as to their progress in building wealth it will also show them the quality of their assets. Do they hold primarily appreciating assets such as a home and/or other real estate? Or, do they hold primarily depreciating assets such as furniture, cars, electronics and other consumer items.

    Calculating and reviewing net worth is an important aspect in and of itself because it will provide a benchmark. It is a check of your child's total financial health. It also provides another important benefit. It helps in goal setting. Much of financial progress can be traced to the setting of goals. In order to make progress in any area of life, goals must be set and effort must be applied to achieve those goals.

    For your child to achieve his net worth goals over time, he will need to work to maximize his income and take advantage of opportunities in his career. He will also need to maximize savings and tackle the ever difficult task of controlling expenses to realize his net worth goals. Forward projections and goals settings are critical to improving your child's net worth. Let's take a look at a simple example.

If your child is 25 years old and finds that he is able to create another $5,000 a year of savings by obtaining a higher paying job and reducing some expenses, the future effect is dramatic.

In the first year, your child will save $5,000. In twenty years, this amount will grow to $33,637 at a 10% annual return. If he should be able to maintain this savings program for a total of 5 years, the total amount of these savings in 20 years will grow to $140,264. This will probably be a dramatic effect on your child's future net worth. Review examples like this with your child so that he sees the tremendous effect of saving today.

Wills, Guardians, Life Insurance, Trusts and Other Fun Topics

You are reading Wealthy Child because you are thinking about the future of your child, grandchild or perhaps both. I believe that it is very hard to help your child or grandchild learn the proper way to handle money and their finances if you don't have your own financial house in order. The primary reason is that children learn primarily by example. You may try as hard as you like to tell your child what he needs to do in life but at the end of the day we will learn from your example. The secondary reason to put your financial life on track is so that your child is not negatively impacted in the years to come by your financial problems. There are plenty of topics that need to be addressed to ensure that your finances are in order and having an updated will is one topic that is not very much fun but needs to be addressed.

It is truly amazing how many people do not have wills. If you own absolutely nothing, then you don't need a will. As most of own at least something we all need a will. Many people will spend hours researching a family vacation or drive to six different stores in an afternoon looking for the best bargain on a gift for their child. These may certainly be rational activities until we realize that some people in this situation do not have a will, or an updated will, in place. It may save $10, $20 or even $500 shopping around for the best deal on a gift or getting the lowest rate on a hotel room for a family vacation but it could cost thousands, tens of thousands or even hundreds of thousands of dollars if a proper, updated will is not in place. A person without a proper will may have to pay estate taxes, probate fees or other attorney fees. Unfortunately, it is not just an issue of cost as it may take your heirs months or years, and cost them precious time, to resolve some of these issues.

No one likes to consider their own death. But, consider this. Consider the fact that you will die at some time. Hopefully, your death is well into the future. No matter when you die do you really want to leave your heirs (often times your children) with a big mess on their hands? This is often what happens when there is no will. A loving and cohesive family may be troubled by arguments and mistrust if there is no will place and each member has thoughts about how mom or dad would have distributed their assets. Make it easy for the loved ones in your life and get a will drawn up by a competent attorney as soon as possible.

Your will is going to stipulate how you would like your assets distributed and any other special conditions. Don't leave your heirs in the dark. Let them know your intentions by writing everything down in a will. There are many, high profile cases each year of people, many of them wealthy and some famous, who die and have no wills. This creates confusion and pain at a time when your survivors should be dealing with their grief and not trying to clean up financial messes.

It is worthwhile to go to a lawyer and a have a will prepared. This way, it will be done correctly. There are boiler plate wills on the internet, but you have no idea whether they are accurate or sufficient. If you are married, make sure that your spouse also has a will. Both parents should have a will in place.

Make sure that your heirs and other trusted people in your life know where you keep your will. They do not need to know what is in the will and they do not necessarily need a copy of your will. However, several people should know where to obtain a copy of your will in the event you die. You can spend a tremendous amount of time and money preparing the world's best will, but if no one can find it when the time comes all of the work and preparation was worthless.

If you have an attorney prepare your will, he or she will usually be willing to keep a copy of your will at their office. You may then give the attorney's business cards to those trusted people that you would like to know how to get a copy of your will if they need to.

If you have young children who cannot take care of themselves in the event you pass away, you'll need to think about what should be done. If there is a surviving spouse then the children will be taken care of. But what if both spouses pass away, perhaps at different times perhaps at the same time, and leave young children behind? To plan for this possibility, you'll need to consider two things.

First, who will be the guardian for your child or children in the event that both parents die? This is not an easy decision and is a very personal one. However, it makes sense to think about this and decide on guardians today. Your chosen guardians will be stipulated in your will. By the way, you should discuss this with the guardians. Don't chose guardians without talking to them first! Believe me, it happens. Second, you'll need to think about how your children will derive financial means with their parents gone. Typically, this involves a trust, a trustee and possibly life insurance.

Let's talk about life insurance first. Unless you have a lot of money, you'll probably need life insurance in the case of your death. This is very important for any parent and sometimes coverage for a non-working spouse many be needed to help defray the cost of childcare expenses.

There continues to be significant debate in the financial planning community these days about what kind of life insurance is best. There is no good answer. One thing is clear. Term Insurance is the purest and cheapest form of life insurance. If you are mostly concerned with providing for your family should you die and you are looking to get the most coverage for the lowest cost, then term insurance is the answer. Term insurance has a specific period of coverage, for example, 10, 20 or 30 years. After the period of the term no coverage is provided and you do not need to pay premiums. Many people who really need term insurance have been sold something other than term life insurance such as whole life insurance. This is usually the case because insurance salespeople receive a much larger commission for selling whole life, and other "permanent" insurance policies, than they do for selling for term insurance.

Trusts are even more complicated than life insurance. It is a shame that these things are so complicated, but that is the way the world works, so there is no point in complaining about it. A trust is an ongoing vehicle that will be funded with some or all of your assets and possibly the payout from any life insurance policies. A trustee will follow what is laid out in the trust but may sometimes have to make decisions as to exactly how something should be done.

Trusts may be used to reduce estate taxes and to direct how assets should be used in the future. We will not discuss the issue of estate taxes here. Directing assets in the future will make sure that your children are taken of and will lessen the chances of an unscrupulous character getting their hands on money that should be for your child's benefit.

Setting up a trust and discussing your specific situation is best done with a competent attorney who is very skilled in these matters. It is a significant investment of time and money but it is well worth it. The satisfaction of knowing that you've done the best for your children should you not be around is peace of mind that is priceless.

There are three other documents that you should consider having as well. They are a health care proxy, a living will and a durable power of attorney. A health care proxy is a legal document used in the United States that names an agent who will make health care decisions in the event that you are unable to make decisions.

A living will lists directives as to the course of treatment you desire in the case you are gravely ill or incapacitated. Some people want to be kept alive at any cost while others only want to be kept alive through extraordinary means if there is a reasonable expectation of recovery. These are very personal and complicated matters. No one will know your wishes and be able to act on them unless you discuss your wishes and then grant this person decision making ability in your living will.

A durable power of attorney names someone who will make decisions (mostly financial and legal) in the event that you are unable to do so because you are either incompetent or incapacitated at the time a decision needs to be made. Again, this is a very complicated area of the law and the only way to address it is to obtain counsel from a qualified attorney.

The Fourteen Rules of Wealth

Below, are the Rules of Wealth. He who follows these rules will become wealthy. Review these lessons with your children as they grow. Make sure they understand why each lesson makes sense. These rules should be reviewed from time to time and your child should think about each rule and how it applies to their financial life.

1) <u>Pay yourself first</u>. Most people receive their paychecks, pay their bills, spend too freely and have nothing left at the end of the week or the month to save. The order is backwards. As your children earn money, make sure that they pay themselves first. When they are young, you may help them do this by having a Savings Box. Fifty percent of all money they earn immediately goes into the Savings Box. As your children get older and receive a regular paycheck, they should use one of the many online banking services (see Appendix D). These online services will take money out of a checking or savings account in any amount and on any day that your child stipulates. If your child is paid $500 on the 1st of each month and has money automatically deposited into his checking account, these banks services will

automatically take a portion and invest it in another account. This account will be your child's "Savings Box" which is never to be touched.

2) <u>The best way to save money is not having a chance to spend it</u>. This is really an extension of Rule 1), Pay yourself first. It doesn't matter how you do it but make sure that money earmarked for savings is quickly and automatically taken from your pay and whisked off to another account or accounts so that you don't have a chance to spend it. If you take advantage of your employer's 401(k), or other similar plan, it will be very hard to get at the money as there is a 10% penalty, in addition to Federal and State income taxes, on any money withdrawn from the account before the age of 59 ½. For all of us, except the most disciplined, the best way to save is to make sure that we never see or get our hands on this money. It is too easy to spend money when it sits in your wallet or in your checking account at the bank. If the money immediately goes into a money market account that is earmarked for some special future purpose you'll be much less likely to spend it. The best situation is one where the account is established so that you are able to wire money in but must show up in person to withdraw money. The more ways you can find to keep from getting at the money the better just as the best way to avoid junk food is not to have any in the house.

3) <u>Save, at all times, at least 10% of your income</u>. You should always strive to save more, but never less than 10%. The more that you earn, the greater the percentage of your income you should save. If your income doubles over the next 10 years and you go from saving 10% to saving 12% something is wrong and you are probably spending too much. If you have scrutinized your expenses from top to bottom and still cannot save 10% of your before tax salary then you should seriously consider obtaining a higher paying job. The future benefit of making this move will be great and will have a very positive impact on your financial situation in the years to come.

4) <u>Increase your income every year</u>. There are many ways to increase one's income. If you become more valuable at work and make a case for your increased value, you will earn more money over time. Create multiple streams of income to increase your total income. Constantly look for opportunities to increase your income and create

multiple streams of income. This is a skill that develops over time and must be practiced. It has been my experience that opportunity does not come knocking. Opportunity usually shows itself and then waits for you to chase it down. The good news is that our ever changing, fast moving and complex economy is producing more opportunity than ever before and technology is allowing individuals to take advantage of this opportunity.

5) <u>Never, ever, ever buy depreciating assets on credit</u>. Not even if the rate offered is 0%! Teach your children to save for the things they want and then pay cash. Have your children live by this rule. These savings, for planned purchases, will be separate and distinct from the money earmarked for your child's Savings Box. Credit should only ever be used to buy appreciating assets. The test is a simple one. You need to ask yourself, "Will I be better off in five years if I buy this?" Depreciating assets will never pass this test as they will be worth less in the future. Wisely bought appreciating assets will always pass the test.

6) <u>Use borrowed money to smartly buy appreciating assets</u>. When you borrow to buy an appreciating asset <u>that you understand</u>, you multiply your returns. For example, if I buy a $100,000 property for cash and it appreciates by 5% a year, I have earned $5,000 or 5% on my money. If I buy a $200,000 property, by borrowing $100,000, and it appreciates by 5% a year, I have earned 10% on my initial $100,000 investment less expenses for the loan. The key is to buy an asset that you truly understand. If you borrow money to buy an asset that loses value, you will be worse off than if you bought it for cash or did not buy it at all.

7) <u>Never, ever, ever withdraw money from a retirement account before the age of 59 ½</u>. Don't do it even if there is a special program that qualifies as an exception, such as buying a house. There is one exception. Anyone who is a billionaire need not pay attention to this rule!

8) <u>Never, ever, ever borrow against a retirement account</u>. The ability to borrow is often pitched as a benefit by plan administrators but at the end of the day, even though you are paying yourself the interest, you are stealing from the future by borrowing today and this

is the opposite of what you should do to become wealthy. There are also usually negative tax consequences in borrowing from a retirement plan.

9) <u>Constantly practice discipline and some denial</u>. Happiness does not come from endlessly buying things. In fact, it has been shown that the life of consumerism seems to make people less happy. The constant chasing of the latest fad, the latest gadget or the latest style provides a short lived high that quickly fades. Learn for yourself, and teach your children, that happiness is not about consuming. It is about living well. Yes, there are items that help us live well, but if we step back and look at what we really need most of us buy too much. We not only buy too many individual items, that we often don't use, but we also pay too much for the items we do buy. Do $100 sneakers really make you feel that much better than a $20 pair? When considering the purchase of an item ask yourself, "Will I truly have the interest and the time to use this item?" Many, many things are purchased and then tucked in the closet never to be used.

10) <u>If it is too good to be true then it is a great deal for the person on the other side of the table and a very bad deal for you</u>. We all want to double or triple our money overnight and this does happen on rare occasions if you are an expert in the area. For every story of someone earning a 1,000% return in one year there are ten thousand stories, never told, of people who lost everything they invested. Do you like odds of 1 in 10,000? I don't.

11) <u>Become involved in a business in some way, shape or form</u>. Find a way to obtain equity. Most wealthy people have some business interests that have substantially added to their wealth. Owning equity in an ongoing business concern is a fantastic way to build substantial wealth.

12) <u>Learn, at least in broad strokes, how the tax code works</u>. Understand why the tax code truly favors business owners and penalizes employees. Employees pay the government first. Business owners pay themselves, and their expenses, first and then they pay the government with whatever is left.

13) <u>Continue your financial education</u>. This should apply to all areas of your life. The world changes and you need to know about potential changes and their effect on your life. Keep up with the latest changes in personal finance as opportunities are constantly created by changes in the economy, changes in the tax code and changes in government policy. If you learn about these changes early on and think about their consequences you may find a great opportunity to increase your financial well being. You also may learn of changes that will negatively impact your wealth if you don't take action. Make sure that you are able to get out of the way in time as these changes often times steamroller those who are unaware.

14) <u>Always take advantage of tax deferred or tax free growth</u>. This is perhaps one of the most powerful methods used in building wealth. A Roth IRA or Roth 401(k) will allow you to contribute after tax money today and then never, ever pay taxes again! If you woke up one day at the age of 60 and had a Roth IRA and a Traditional IRA and each had $1 million you should realize that you have two very different assets. If you decided to withdraw the $1 million from the Traditional IRA you would get to keep about $600,000 after paying taxes. If you withdrew $1 million from your Roth IRA you would get to keep nearly $1 million as no Federal income taxes would be due. This is the power of tax free growth!

Tax deferred growth is almost as good as tax free growth and certainly far better than taxable growth.

Appendix A: The Nickel Game

Week One:

On Monday, there is 1 nickel on the table.

On Tuesday, there are 2 nickels on the table.

On Wednesday, there are 4 nickels on the table.

On Thursday, there are 8 nickels on the table.

On Friday, there are 16 nickels on the table.

On Saturday, there are 32 nickels on the table.

On Sunday, there are 64 nickels on the table.

At the end of week one, 1 nickel has grown to 64 nickels or $3.20.

Week Two:

On Monday, there are 128 nickels which is $6.40.

On Tuesday, there are 256 nickels which is $12.80.

On Wednesday, there are 512 nickels which is $25.60.

On Thursday, there are 1,024 nickels which is $51.20.

On Friday, there are 2,048 nickels which is $102.40.

On Saturday, there are 4,096 nickels which is $204.80.

On Sunday, there are 8,192 nickels which is $409.60.

After two weeks, 1 nickel has grown to $409.60. Discuss with your child that this is what happens when you invest your money and it grows by compounding. This is one of the most important lessons that your child may learn as it is one of the most powerful tools in finance.

Also show your children the flip side of compounding, i.e. what would a sum of money be worth in the future if your child _decided to save it today rather than spend it_. For example, at a 10% annual growth, $100, if not spent on a toy now, would be worth $161 in 5 years and $259 in 10 years.

Appendix B: Historical Return of Equities by Sector

In everyday conversation about the stock market people talk about and refer to "the market" as if the stock market were one, homogenous group of stocks. This is not entirely correct. The stock market is very much like a large stream. A stream seems like one entity. It is after all just water collected in one place. Closer inspection shows that different parts of the stream may behave very differently from other parts of the stream.

Some parts of the stream have little to no life and may have still water with a sandy bottom with no plants. Other parts of the stream may have fast moving water with lots of food passing by, many fish and other plants. If you were to visit one part of the stream it may look nothing like another part of the stream. The same is true of the stock market.

It has been astutely observed that the stock market is really a "market of stocks" and it must be remembered that any particular stock represents shares within a particular company. Google stock is very different from Disney stock which is very different from General Motors stock. They are in different businesses, are growing at different rates and each have their own "company culture." All of these factors affect their business and their stock price over time.

The overall stock market may have a year to date return of 10% but there will be plenty of individual stocks that show a return that is better or worse than 10%. In addition, the stock market may be broken down into particular sectors. For example, companies that sell food products all tend to act in roughly the same way in response to economic conditions. Different sectors tend to perform well at different times during an economic cycle. Sometimes sectors are grouped together into what are called indexes or indices. For example, most of us have heard of the Dow Jones Index or the NASDAQ. The creators of these indices had an aim in mind when constructing the index. For example, the NASDAQ index was constructed mainly of technology and other companies that are seen as being innovative and on the forefront of the economy. Keep in mind that there are also other stock markets around the world. There are stock markets in Japan, Brazil, Russia and many other countries. These also count when we talk about the stock market. They often behave slightly differently, and sometimes very differently, from the stock market in the United States.

The point is that the stock market is comprised of many different parts and these parts perform differently over time. To be properly diversified you'll need to ensure that you have your stock market investment spread broadly across sectors and that you don't have too much exposed to one particular area or only a few areas of the stock market.

While most of us enjoy investing at home it will be more and more important in the future to invest abroad to capture the faster growth that is occurring in other parts of the world such as South and Central America, Asia and Russia. These stock markets can certainly fluctuate more than the stock market in the United States but they benefit from faster underlying economic growth which is a long term recipe for higher stock market returns over time. There are many very good mutual funds and Exchange Traded Funds (ETFs) that will allow you to invest in these fast growing countries.

The difference between being invested in a sector that performs well over a 20 year period and a sector that doesn't could easily mean the difference between having another $1 million in a retirement account. While it is impossible to know which sectors will outperform others in the future there are certain trends that you can identify that will have a better chance of growing more quickly than others.

Appendix C: Resources for Establishing a Business Entity

It is easier today than at any other time to establish a business entity. You will need to think about the business and consult with a competent advisor to determine what structure suits the business best. There are pros and cons to each structure and the tax consequences vary as well. Your tax advisor and attorney will best be able to determine how best to address your needs. In any case, a business usually provides favorable tax treatment and is something that you can call your own and take pride in building.

A business may be established as a sole proprietorship, a corporation (there are different kinds), a Limited Partnership (LP), Limited Liability Company (LLC) among other options. An attorney will be able to help you in setting up whatever structure suits your business and your personal situation best. If you feel comfortable making this decision yourself and are willing to take advantage of a lower cost option you may want to forgo an attorney and use a firm that specializes in helping "do it yourselfers" in setting up a business entity.

There are many firms that will help you with the paperwork. These firms will file the necessary paperwork with the relevant government agencies to ensure that your company is properly established. They will also handle any ongoing filings for a yearly fee. Please note that in most cases they will not file the paperwork necessary for income tax filings. This will need to be done by you or your tax advisor. Below, is a brief list of several of the larger companies that will assist you in establishing an entity for your business.

The Company Corporation www.corporate.com

Legal Zoom www.LegalZoom.com

Companies Incorporated www.companiesinc.com

BizFilings www.BizFilings.com

Inc-It-Now www.inc-it-now.com

My Corporation www.mycorporation.com

Appendix D: Establishing an Online Bank Account

One of the truisms of wealth building is that your child must pay himself before anyone else while he is working. One of the best ways to do this is to have money automatically taken out of his regular checking account and whisked away to another account that makes it more difficult to withdraw the money. While it can be almost impossible to adhere to a budget and then attempt to save what is leftover at the end of the month, experience has shown that people generally confine their spending to the available money they have for the month. Hence, it makes perfect sense to have your savings taken care of first and then spend what is left. Online banks have made this easier than ever.

The money should be taken from your child's regular savings account as soon as possible after his paycheck is deposited. Since many companies pay their employees via ACH (meaning there is no paper check that your child needs to deposit) the money is sent to your child's checking account on a particular day each pay period. Let's say that your child's take home pay is $2,000 per month. Your child should strive to save at least 10% of this, or $200, per month. If your child is paid on the 14th and 28th of each month, $1,000 on each date, he should setup an online bank account to save $100 on the 14th and $100 on the 28th. Then, your child will have $1,800 to spend during the month.

There are many reputable institutions that will allow you or your child to easily establish an online bank account and link it to an existing checking account. Here are just a few:

ING Direct www.ingdirect.com

HSBC Direct www.hsbcdirect.com

A search of Google for online banks will yield many more. Personally, I have had a very good experience with ING Direct over the years.

Once the online bank account is established your child will need to enter his current checking account information which will include the ABA routing number and the account number. This information is shown on the bottom of each check and is a string of numbers. Then, he will need to enter the dates on which he would like funds taken from his existing checking account to the online account and the amount. Then, your child's automatic savings plan is in place!

Please don't forget to have your child setup an automatic contribution plan for the Roth IRA, if eligible, or the Traditional IRA if your child is not eligible for the Roth IRA.

Appendix E: Buying Individual Stocks

It used to be that buying stock in a particular company, rather than an equity mutual fund which contains many, many different stocks, was rather expensive because of the commission by a broker to do so was high. This has changed dramatically in the last ten years and an individual is now able to purchase 100 or 1,000 shares of stock in a publicly held company for as little as $5! The problem today is not the high cost of the commission the problem is having the knowledge to properly buy the right stocks at the right time.

The traditional wisdom, which I tend to agree with, is that your child should look into purchasing individual stocks only after he or she has a decent sum of money broadly invested in the stock market in a well diversified manner. For example, if your child has $15,000 broadly invested in the stock market through index mutual funds or ETFs then he may look into buying individual stocks.

Buying individual stocks is a learning experience that will require significant education and ongoing learning. There are many, many good books on the topics and several periodicals. I highly recommend Investors Business Daily (IBD). This daily newspaper is based on a strategy designed by William O'Neill. Mr. O'Neill's strategy is certainly not the only way to invest in single stocks but his paper provides a fantastic education for those interested in purchasing stocks.

Appendix F: Establishing a UTMA or UGMA

     If you have a young child or children in your life putting money away for them early on and then teaching them about saving and investing will go a long way to helping them succeed financially. One of the best ways to do this is to establish a UTMA or UGMA in their name with you as the custodian. You should establish the account at a brokerage firm so that you may purchase mutual funds, ETFs and single stocks. Young children should take advantage of maximum growth and need heavy equity exposure.

     Contact the brokerages that you have a relationship with and check their fees related to such an account and any minimum account size required.

Appendix G: ETFs vs. Mutual Funds

Mutual funds have been a fantastic way to invest by allowing average investors to easily diversify and have a full time mutual fund manager pick investments and manage the fund. Of course, for this management you, as the investor, generally pay a yearly fee of somewhere between .05% and 3% of the balance you have in the mutual fund. The most common yearly fee is around 1.2%. On a $10,000 mutual fund investment 1.2% is $120 per year. In the past few years, ETFs have become, in some cases, a better alternative to mutual funds.

An Exchange Traded Fund (ETF) is very much like a mutual fund, trades throughout the day, instead of simply having an end of day price, and is usually cheaper than a comparable mutual fund.

ETFs may be bought and sold if you have a brokerage account and are starting to become available within 401(k) and other retirement plans. In the near future you will see more and more ETFs being offered and will become more readily available in many different types of retirement plans.

In discussing investments always be sure to ask if there is an ETF alternative to any mutual fund that may be offered to you. Keep in mind that there are usually ETFs that exactly match any index mutual fund. In other cases there will be similar ETFs for some mutual funds. In many cases there is no comparable ETF for a particular mutual fund. In this case you need to decide whether the additional cost of that mutual fund is worth it.

About the Author

William A. Gerosa holds a Bachelor of Arts from Boston University in Economics and an MBA in Finance from Columbia University. He has worked for Bloomberg Financial Markets, Citigroup, Deutsche Bank and nabCapital as Head of Market Risk for the Americas.

Bill has started or been involved in several businesses since the age of twelve. His venture, www.GroWWealthy.com, helps people help themselves with money and wealth by offering suggestions, showing how to earn, keep and grow money and providing easy to follow tips and advice for improving one's financial health. Visit www.GroWWealthy.com for more information.

www.ingramcontent.com/pod-product-compliance
Lightning Source LLC
Chambersburg PA
CBHW022102160426
43198CB00008B/316